WILHELM
REICH
A Personal Biography

WILHELM REICH

A Personal Biography
by Ilse Ollendorff Reich

*with an introduction
by Paul Goodman*

ST. MARTIN'S PRESS / NEW YORK / 1969

ST. MARTIN'S PRESS INC.
175 Fifth Avenue New York NY 10010

THE MACMILLAN COMPANY OF CANADA LIMITED
70 Bond Street Toronto 2

For Eva, Lore, and Peter

Acknowledgments

I wish to express my appreciation to all those who actively helped me with the task of collecting the necessary background material. My special thanks go to A. S. Neill and Dr. Ola Raknes who put their voluminous correspondence with Reich at my disposal in addition to generously offering their time for many talks about Reich; to Dr. Annie Reich, Jo Jenks, and Gladys Meyer Wolfe who contributed reminiscences and photographs; to Elsa Lindenberg for her willingness to share her memories of Reich with me; and to all the many others who contributed notes, letters, and memories and thus helped to make this a more rounded picture of the man Reich.

Contents

List of Illustrations

Introduction

I asked a group of American radical students about Wilhelm Reich, and no one had heard of him. A dozen years ago he would have been one of their major heroes and strongest influences. Apparently it has been that easy for official suppression and a kind of conspiracy of silence by his scientific peers to drive a great man (temporarily) out of sight. Yet the repressed always return, with a new aura, and the signs are that, beginning in Europe, Reich is returning.

More than any other figure of our times, Reich has had things to say—and do—essential for the chief revolutionary actions of the young, whether their politics or their hippie life style; indeed, he is the connecting link between these contrasting tendencies. The most trenchant political ideas of Marcuse and Fromm, about the fear of freedom and the co-opting of spontaneity and sexuality by modern corporate institutions, were stated first and more powerfully by Reich. And he was able to demonstrate the material and efficient causes involved, e.g. in incomplete gratification, anxiety, and introjection, whereas the others are rather abstract. Conversely, Reich would not have been surprised, as Marcuse has been, at the theoretically "impossible" youth revolt, for it was in the cards for the children of affluence, brought up without toilet training, freely masturbating, and with casual clothing, to be daring, disobedient, and simple-minded. Human nature is very malleable, but there are material facts that cannot be altogether co-opted.

Self-regulation and the cosmic streaming that relaxes and transcends ego are axioms of the hippie way. Here again, in vegetotherapy, Reich invented a practical yoga in familiar Western terms and without drugs, so that it is possible to tune in without dropping out, without having to lose one's wits, although of course not without conflict and suffering. And these exercises are a fundamental part of the sensitivity training and Artaudian theater which are prevalent. Similarly, Reich is an existential psychologist, but unlike the others he does not have to rely on extreme situations and peak experiences, but can make something of the everyday.

Reich's work ethic, the human need for absorption in productive work that is one's own and gets one beyond oneself, does not sit so well with the radical young, for it is true that the majority of professions and economic jobs are corrupted and often useless or worse. Yet this Lutheran doctrine of justification by vocation is probably true, and Reich's work democracy *is* the decentralized "participatory democracy" that the radical young hanker after, though they have not thought through the meaning of work. Doing one's thing is not a whimsical way of being in the world. Reich here went back to the young-Marxian conception of actual alienation in the work process, which the later Marx tended to forget, as he became a more formal sociologist and politician. (My guess is that Reich's glancing references to anarchist thinkers as a source for these ideas stem solely from a single conversation with myself.) In his own life and work, to be sure, Reich was obsessional and Calvinistic about work; he was driven by his furies. I think he over-estimated the power of the paraphernalia of the laboratory and methodical science to solve humanistic problems. And he was a very autocratic democrat.

In the following pages we see that Ilse Ollendorff could not "follow" her husband in his later researches, and this raises the question of what kind of great man Reich was. It is important to spell out what the issue is here. For whether or not the theory of the orgone is exact physics, it was certainly a courageous new attempt to fulfill the human conviction that there must be a connection between natural energy and psychiatric depths. Thus, as the older magical religions have lapsed or become superficial, young people have inevitably gravitated to every kind of sacramental theory and sacramentalism, from Jung and the *Book of Changes* to LSD; but it seems to me that Reich was on a more likely, arduous, track. If, of course, the orgone indeed exists as he told it, he was its Franklin, Volta, and Faraday rolled into one, and the consequences are extraordinary for physiology and religion. But even if it is only analogy and projection, it is not mere raving but is in the great line of the archaic chemists and Paracelsus, groping toward what must be fact in the long run. This kind of gigantic error is abounding in truth.

A teasing dilemma of such physico-psychiatric theories is the inevitable ambiguity of replication of experiments, because at these depths what is perceived depends on the power and openness of the perceiving and therefore the character of the perceiver. So among the earnest alchemists Christian virtue was a prerequisite for the researcher, or the experiment turned to catastrophe. (One cannot help thinking of this in reading of Reich's DOR experiment.) Work in parapsychology is similarly bedevilled by the difficulty of élite observers. I do not mean to assert the paradox that Important Experiments can be replicated only by Chosen People, but there does seem to be a limitation in principle to the objectivity of science as ordinarily understood—there is a sociology, psychology, and theology of science which is *not* irrelevant to what is discovered.

How one is determines not only what one looks for but also, partly, what one can see. As Augustine said, one must love in order to learn. So far as I know, let me hasten to say, Reich himself held no such view, but maybe he should have held it.

Ilse Ollendorff's "personal biography" is a unique document, a frank and reasonable account of how it is to be near, day in day out, a great and problematic person. Despite obvious storm and stress and what must have been bitter hurt feelings, she disciplines herself to an account that is feelingful but dispassionate. There is no backbiting. Her reticence about her troubles with Reich's disciples and the estate is admirably correct, since every such conflict has two sides, and now what difference does it make? More remarkable is her immense respect for him, as was his due, at the same time as she is not swallowed up by him. She is intelligent and independent and not presumptuous. The one serious lapse in her account is her silence about their sexual relations; this is understandable, but I do not think it was necessary.

What comes through poignantly is the solitude of this man, perhaps of any great man. She does not reveal it deliberately; it comes through as a fact of everyday existence. Typically, she describes his habits in driving a car and how he glowers at deviant motorists, but we do not learn what he was like when he was deep in thought, inspired, beautiful. This does not mean that she was unaware, but simply that when a great man is being great, the others are under a spell, and this leaves him high and dry. Conversely, those who glowingly tell us about such things are usually precisely not independent, not friends. Maybe Neill was an exception, but he was far away.

Though competent to judge, his wife is unwilling to say how mad Reich was or became. No doubt he was somewhat mad, but the interesting question, of course, is in what areas and to what degree. I assume that she does not know. It is certainly significant that she can do without the idea, she does not have to make an issue of it. His written outpourings of rage and grief are often of a man at his wit's end, but not out of his wits, and not unjustified, the world being what it is. Much so-called madness is the desperate response to the double-binds of an absurd environment, and we all have plenty of that.

What strikes me, indeed, is not evidence of abnormal derangement but how he harassed himself, wasted himself, and suffered by falling victim to a characteristic of our society, and of scientific society, that is now judged eminently normal. This was his compulsion to organize Institutes, to be a Public Scientist, a political influence, to be allied with Higher Powers (including the United States Air Force), to be busy with the Cold War like countless other maniacs, although he was an explorer and a loner, and a physician of souls. It is clear enough how the social conditions of our times drive, or entice, gifted people into this kind of ambivalence; but it is an impossible way of life nevertheless. And then, in disastrous counterpoint to this internal contradiction, is the melancholy history of expulsions, continually being a refugee, struggling to get visas and to satisfy bureaucrats.

Paul Goodman

Oceanic Institute
Waimanalo, Hawaii

AUTHOR'S PREFACE

For many years, whenever I talked with friends and acquaintances about my years with Reich I was told to put these things down on paper, and I have played with the idea of writing a biography for a long time, without really taking it seriously. Now that I am tackling this job in earnest, I regret that I did not write down much more over the years than I actually have.

I met Reich in October 1939 shortly after his arrival in the States. I became his wife, secretary, laboratory assistant, bookkeeper, housekeeper, and general factotum soon thereafter, the mother of his son in 1944, and was closely associated with him and his work until our separation in 1954. Even after our separation we kept in close personal contact because of our mutual concern about our son and each other's well-being, although I deliberately kept away from his work from that time on for reasons that will become apparent later.

This biography will necessarily be a subjective one, because all the data that I have been able to gather, all the conversations I had with many of Reich's old friends and co-workers, in fact, all the material that I have collected becomes reinterpreted by me in my way of seeing Reich and remembering him. In the course of collecting the material I was often made to realize how tricky one's memory can be. The same occurrence, as related to me by several people would often take on a great variety of conflicting detail; in the process, my own memories would become uncertain. In many such cases, I have finally just presented the various interpretations of my several sources and left it to the reader to choose that which he thinks is the most likely.

I have absolutely no access to any of the material contained in the archives of the Wilhelm Reich Infant Trust Fund, the organization in charge of Reich's estate. Among the archives are Reich's diaries which he kept regularly since his student days in Vienna, photographs and correspondence, and some unpublished and unfinished writings. According to Reich's Last Will and Testament, the stipulation that the archives be locked away for fifty years after his death applies to all of the material; therefore it will be left to future biographers to verify and correct some of the facts I present.

I have also been denied access to the library at the Orgone Energy Observatory in Rangeley, Maine. It would have given me valuable clues as to Reich's specific interests at various times in his life. This library has been kept more or less intact since Reich left Vienna in 1930, traveling with him to Berlin, Sweden, Norway, and the United States. Since Reich was in the habit of marking everything that caught his interest in a book or magazine, it would have been very interesting to see, for instance, in the old editions of Karl Kraus's revolutionary periodical *Die Fackel* (The Torch), how much influence some of the articles had on Reich's own political development.

Thus the material available for this biography consisted of my own memory; the many letters my son Peter and I have from Reich; notes that were kept by Reich's students; the correspondence that some old friends, particularly A. S. Neill and Ola Raknes, have put at my disposal; the many conversations I have had with friends and former associates of Reich's here in the United States, as well as in England, Germany and Norway; and of some biographical material previously published.

I very definitely regard my attempt as a preliminary biography only. I am neither a scientist nor a psychiatrist, and I will have to leave it to future scientists to write an evaluation of Reich's scientific work, just as it will have to be left to people trained in the field of depth psychology to interpret Reich's life and work from their point of view. I can write about things only as I have experienced them, as I understood them, and as I feel about them.

My intention is to retell Reich's life as I knew it, and as I can best reconstruct it, to show somewhat how events and times influenced his life and work, and how he, in turn, helped to shape the minds of his contemporaries. I do not intend to defend him or his actions, nor to whitewash him; neither do I nor can I judge him or his work. By retracing his development, I hope to gain a better understanding of the man Reich, to bring him closer to people so that they may understand what drove him and why he became such a tragic figure.

What kind of man was Reich? To some he was a hero who could do no wrong and who was above human faults and weaknesses; to others he was "that mad scientist;" but to all, without a doubt, he was a genius. In my research, talking to friends and foes of Reich, one thing stands out above all others: his great vitality. It was always mentioned first, the outstanding quality of the man in whatever connection, his elan, his energy, his almost overpowering strength. Without it he could not have survived the many emigrations, the repeated loss of home, livelihood, organizational connections. Each time he recovered, determined not to let it get him down, the eternal optimist; as he once put it, the eternal *Stehaufmännchen.*

He was a man of great contradictions, and I think that the pictures of him at the end of the illustration section show his different sides very clearly. One is the gentle, naïve, almost childlike man of whom Nic Waal, one of his Norwegian co-workers and friends, in the memorial volume *Wilhelm Reich* said "he had the true innocence and restless searching mind of the creator." He was gentle with children—all through his life he maintained a wonderful immediate contact with children—and he was patient when he felt a situation or person required patience. But he could be the stern, impatient, awe-inspiring person of the final picture, especially with his assistants and co-workers. I think he never understood that people, in general, did not have the same energy and vitality that he had, and he expected from everyone the same single-mindedness of purpose and ability to work and create. He felt frustrated, irritated, and let down if people did not produce and work the way he did. He often drove people mercilessly, and lost many good workers because they could not meet his pace.

His mind was incredibly quick to grasp new facts and ideas, and once something was clear to him, he expected everybody else to understand it too—another source of frustration and impatience if it did not happen. In many of his writings, especially the later ones, he presupposes knowledge in the reader of facts or theories that are obvious to him; he seems to jump and leave gaps, making the material appear, to my mind, more difficult and disconnected than it in fact is.

Most people who were in close contact with Reich were aware of the gap between their ability and his, and reacted to it with willing acceptance, sometimes with absolute hero worship, or they withdrew, often in anger and frustration. But no matter what their reaction was, it seems clear to me that no one who for any length of time was in Reich's orbit was left untouched by him.

There is another way people saw Reich that must be mentioned here. Many people upon hearing his name still respond, "Oh, that man who was obsessed by sex," implying that there is something not quite proper or serious about a scientist who is interested in sex. To Reich, sex was to be equated with life per se. He often said that sex was one of the most neglected aspects of life, no one dared touch upon it or mention it, even in science, and even after Freud. Because he felt it to be one of the most powerful and influential aspects of human life, Reich made it for a long time the center of his scientific investigation. To many people, that seemed to make him "obsessed by sex." Whenever anyone tried to attack him for his discoveries or his research in other fields, his work on sexuality was pulled in, out of context, and used to debase him in one way or another. The obsession with sex, with pornography, was in the critics' mind. Reich detested pornography, dirty jokes, and all perversions of sexuality. I never heard him tell a dirty joke. For him sex and love were one. His motto was, "Love, Work and Knowledge are the wellsprings of our life. They should also govern it," and in his ideal world of the future these three aspects of life were to be equally balanced, as he wanted them to be in his own life.

How did Reich see himself? We can, of course, judge only from his writings and spoken words. I think he looked upon himself more as a natural scientist than as a physician. He felt hundreds of years ahead of his times, and often said that it did not matter if he were not recognized in his lifetime, that he would be known through his work five hundred or a thousand years hence. He felt that his discoveries put him in a class with Galileo or Giordano Bruno, and he took his very real persecutions as the inevitable fate of every great discoverer. He repeatedly said that if one dealt with explosive matters, such as the Life Energy, one had to expect explosive reactions.

In his later years, he undoubtedly began to identify more and more with Christ whose true message, he thought, was distorted by his disciples, and he feared the same would happen to his work. Reich knew he was alone, that nobody could really follow him in his ideas, but he found it very hard to accept this fact that he was, as he put it, "outside the trap." The quotation from Isaac Newton that Reich put at the end of his book *People in Trouble* gives an indication of how he saw himself.

> I do not know what I may appear to the world; but to myself I seem to have been only like a boy playing on the seashore, and diverting myself in now and then finding a smoother pebble or a prettier shell than ordinary whilst the great ocean of truth lay all undiscovered before me.

I think it is too early for us to attempt an evaluation of Reich's own judgment about himself, but I have no doubt that he was a great man and that his influence is being felt in much of present-day thinking and writing.

Early Years

All the facts we know about Reich's early childhood are those he told his family and friends, and he did not talk too much or too often about his childhood. We know that he was born on March 24, 1897, in Dobrzcynica, in that part of Galicia which belonged to the Austrian Empire. His father's family, as he told me once, had a famous wise rabbi among its members; however his father was no longer a faithful Jew but rather had become assimilated, spoke only German with his children and his wife, and did not give his children a Jewish religious education. Reich's mother, Cecilia Roniger, came from that part of Austria which belongs now to Roumania.

Soon after Wilhelm Reich's birth, the family moved to the

1

Ukrainian part of Austria, to Jujinetz in the Bukovina. From members of the family I could ascertain that the family was well-to-do, highly respected, somewhat stuck-up, and put a very pronounced stress on German culture. There were uncles on both sides of the family who were representatives in the Austrian Congress, and others who were professional men. The new farm in the Bukovina was a large estate bought with the financial help of some of the relatives, but eventually owned by Reich's father alone. The family at that time consisted of father, mother, Wilhelm, and Robert who was three years younger than Wilhelm. The father raised mainly beef cattle on the large estate, and had a contract with the German government for army meat supply which at one time required a trip to Berlin. Mother accompanied the father on that occasion, and her buying a dress in Berlin, together with the trip, became a much talked about event in the family.

The father has been described as a rather brutal man, with feudal attitudes toward his fieldhands and family, given to violent temper outbursts, but very much in love with his wife and very jealous of other men's interest in her. The mother, judging from the pictures, was a highly attractive woman, but seems to have been much subdued by her husband. She is reported as having been rather unintellectual and not very clever, a good housewife, and her own mother, Grandmother Roniger, is known to have talked about her as *das Schaf* (the lamb) which in German very definitely has the connotation of "the dumb one."

There are no childhood companions that we can consult about the life of the family on the farm. Reich said on many occasions that he was left very much to his own devices, that he had few playmates since he was not allowed to associate with either the Ukrainian peasant children or the Yiddish-speaking children of the few Jewish families in the nearby village. I have always found it surprising that under these circumstances, when the two brothers must have been thrown together a great deal, Reich talked very little about his brother. In fact, some of his old friends did not even know that he had a brother and were surprised when I mentioned him. It is true the brother died at the rather early age of twenty-six, but Reich's relationship with his brother is nonetheless one of the puzzling factors of his childhood. One of Reich's Viennese friends who had met the brother during Reich's student days described him as looking like a weak copy of Reich. In the picture that I have seen of Robert at twenty-five years of age he shows a definite family resemblance, but appears to be a more gentle person than Reich. In talks with Robert's widow I was able to find out some interesting facts about the relationship of the two brothers. Both were bright and seemed to have been in competition with each other from the very beginning. As Reich told it, as a boy he had wanted not a brother, but a sister; when informed of the birth of a brother, he said that he was not interested and that they could take him right back. The brothers seem to have been in competition for the love of their mother, and both claimed to be the favorite of their old cook Sosha, each contending that she always made only his favorite dishes. Even in later years, when reminiscing about their childhood, the element of competition was always present, each claiming to have been the better horseman or the better hunter. (Reich, according to his own stories, was a rather wild youngster. He loved horses, and learned to ride very early.) Both brothers seemed to have acquired the father's tendency toward violent temper outbursts, and one would often react to such outbursts in the other with the remark "you behave like Father," which came close to being an insult.

All through his life Reich idolized his mother. No other woman's cooking over the years, for example, could ever reach her perfection. Elsa Lindenberg, Reich's second wife, told me that she was never able to make an apple strudel just like his mother used to make, and no matter how hard I tried I could never produce a special cabbage dish that he liked exactly the way his mother had made it. I once came very close to it when I slightly burned the cabbage, and ever since I have had my private doubts about Mrs. Reich's perfection as a cook.

Reich's father was a great hunter, and taught Reich very early how to handle a gun. Although in his later life Reich could not bear the idea of hunting for sport, he enjoyed target shooting and the feel of a good gun in his hand. He kept a small collection of guns at Orgonon in Maine, and taught our son Peter very early the art of handling a gun correctly.

Reich talked very little about his relationship with his father. I have the feeling that it was a very ambivalent relationship, because on more than one occasion Reich tried to imply that he was not really his father's son, that maybe his mother had a relationship with one of the Ukrainian peasants—a rather unlikely story for that time and place—and in the end, went so far as to offer the even more unlikely proposition that he was the offspring of his mother and a man from outer space. Whatever the situation was, the father was concerned enough about his son to take him to Vienna for medical consultation and therapy when young Willie developed on one of his elbows a severe excema that would not yield to the usual medication by the village doctor. The child stayed at one of the Vienna hospitals for six weeks, but in spite of early diagnosis and medication he continued to suffer from this skin condition for the rest of his life.

As Reich has written, he received his schooling at home from tutors who prepared him for entrance in the German *Gymnasium* at Czernowitz (Cernauti) at the age of fourteen. Shortly before this, he suffered the most severe trauma of his early years through the death of his mother by suicide. To my mind, this event became one of the most crucial forces in his life.

There seems to be little doubt from what I could gather in my talks with Reich, his family, and some close friends, that he played a role in his mother's death by revealing her love affair with one of the tutors to his father. That Reich was unable to resolve this question may be one reason why he was never able to successfully finish his own analysis; there were certain problems that he was never able to face.

The father, according to family reports, was so devastated by the death of the mother that only the thought of his two sons kept him from taking his own life. He insured his life heavily and afterward contracted pneumonia, standing for hours in cold weather in a pond, ostensibly fishing. The pneumonia developed into tuberculosis and he died in 1914. (The life insurance for his sons was never recovered; Reich consequently became so suspicious of any kind of life insurance that in later life he would never consider taking out a policy for the protection of his own family.)

Before his father's death Reich lived as a boarding student with a family in Czernowitz while going to the *Gymnasium,* spending his vacations at the farm helping his father. After his father's death Reich took over his father's work while continuing his studies. He passed his *Abiturium* in 1915, *mit Stimmeneinhelligkeit* (with

unanimous approval) and, as his homeland had become a battle-
field, he joined the Austrian army in which he became an officer
in 1916. His brother was sent to Vienna to live with relatives.

Reich often spoke with a certain nostalgia of his childhood years
on the farm. He remembered especially the young Ukrainian girls
who were his nursemaids, their earthiness, and the warmth with
which they cuddled him. He remembered the folk songs they used
to sing, and the folk dances in which he sometimes participated.
He told of the large fishponds where carp were raised, and although he liked to eat freshly caught freshwater fish, he never
liked fishing, and thought of it as a cruel sport. He used to say
that it always made him think of a great big giant dangling a juicy
steak in front of a human, only to hook the poor human on a sharp
barb the moment he was tempted to take a bite. He remembered
riding for hours over the fields, surveying the harvest, and enjoying the smell of the fields, and the newmown hay. But he never
went back to the farm after leaving it to join the army.

There are a few photographs in the archives which Reich sometimes would look through with us, showing him as a dashing
young officer in the Austrian army. He wore a small mustache,
and was a very handsome young man, indeed. I think, on the
whole, he enjoyed his military life. He was not a pacifist by nature,
and the responsibility for a group of people was much to his liking.
He saw active duty on the Italian front, and sometimes told how
they were shelled for days at a time, dashing out of a shelter one
by one at certain counts to get food and supplies. He remembered
the very cooperative Italian girls who taught him a smattering of
Italian, and he blamed one unhappy episode, when he was stuck
for three days in a swampy ditch, for a renewed outbreak of his
skin condition that was never to be completely cured.

He must have liked wearing an officer's uniform. He told us
that even though he was in the infantry, he always wore spurs,
and that on his rare furloughs he loved to go riding at the Vienna
Reitschule.

I have a feeling that at that time his social conscience was not
very developed, and that he took the war in stride without bothering much about the rights and wrongs. He was, up to that time,
certainly no rebel.

Vienna: 1918–1930

Having returned from the war to Vienna at the end of 1918, Reich first matriculated at the Faculty of Law of the University of Vienna. But he soon became dissatisfied with the dryness of his studies, their remoteness from human affairs, and switched, even before the end of the first semester, to the Faculty of Medicine. As a war veteran he was given the privilege of working at a faster pace than the general medical student, and was able to compress six years of medical studies into four.

In these first years of studies, Reich shared a small apartment with his brother Robert and another student. After his return from the war, the brothers had decided that Willie should study first, while Robert worked to earn some of the money needed for their upkeep, and that later on Willie would provide for Robert's studies. They were desperately poor and hungry. A friend of theirs recalls finding a note pinned to their icebox saying, "Willie, I left a dish of potatoes, but don't eat them all, leave some for Robert."

Fellow students remember that he had no civilian suit and wore his uniform and miltiary coat to classes. He got the necessary instruments and books through loans and gifts from the Vienna Medical Society. One of his co-students and friends tells of bringing double portions of sandwiches to the university for his lunch —to the great astonishment of her mother who could not understand her slim daughter's ravenous appetite and attributed it to a *Bandlwurm* (tapeworm). Another friend remembers that the psychoanalyst Dr. Paul Federn often invited Reich for meals at his home, first because he enjoyed the conversation with the young student, but also because he wished to provide him with some necessary nourishment. After the first semesters, however, Reich managed to earn some money coaching other students in the subjects he had just finished.

The same friend who provided the sandwiches also relates that Reich's driving energy, his quickness of mind, and his expectation that everybody should be just like him were already very much in evidence. She recalls that she was still dissecting a finger in anatomy when Reich was dissecting a brain, and how impatient he grew when she was not able to follow his work in detail. At that time he discovered skiing, quickly became expert in it, and invited her to ski with him. But as she was a novice and had to stay on the practice slopes, he abandoned her there and went off on his trails, apparently not giving her a second thought. She recalls that in general he was an outstanding student, a leader in student discussions, liked by many but disliked by others because of his brilliance.

In 1919, one of his fellow students invited him to attend a lecture on psychoanalysis. The subject matter impressed him to such an extent that he soon decided to devote his life to psychiatry. He brought such enthusiasm, energy, and interest to the then fairly new and revolutionary concepts of psychoanalysis that he was allowed to join the Vienna Psychoanalytic Society as an undergraduate medical student, a rather unusual distinction. His first paper, written under the influence of psychoanalytic thought, was called "Ibsen's Peer Gynt, Libidokonflikte und Wahngebilde" (libido conflicts and hallucinations). It was never published, but Reich did, on occasion, refer to it in conversations.

He received his medical degree from the University of Vienna in 1922, and then continued his training as psychiatrist for two more years under Professors Wagner-Jauregg and Paul Schilder. When he later spoke of his studies at the university, he remembered with special pleasure the biology lectures given by Professor Paul Kammerer whom he credited with his continuing interest in biology. If I remember rightly, he used to say that the only aspects of his medical studies he disliked were forensic medicine and pharmaceutic medicine.

Another dimension which he discovered in these early student years was the world of music. He joined the Schoenberg Verein (Society). He had had piano lessons as a child, and according to Annie Reich, his first wife, had played the cello before she met him. His friendship with Rudolf Kolisch, the well-known violinist, brother-in-law of Schoenberg, dates from these days and was later renewed in the United States. In later years Reich loved to play the piano and still later the organ. His taste in music was rather conservative. He loved Beethoven above all, especially the symphonies; he enjoyed Mozart and Haydn and most of the romantic composers, but had little interest in Bach and baroque music. One of his special favorites was Brahms's *Alto Rhapsodie* as sung by Marian Anderson, but in general he thought that Brahms's music was too Germanic, too professorial. I also remember his endless—and fruitless—heated discussions with his friend and colleague Dr. Theodore Wolfe in New York in the forties. They argued about the respective merits of Beethoven and Bach, neither one ever able to convince the other of the superiority of his musical hero.

When we later moved—in 1941—to a larger house in Forest Hills, Reich was able to find a very good secondhand Steinway Grand, and he used to play often, always his own fantasies which were pleasant to listen to, rather sentimental and romantic, and somewhat commonplace. Later on, at Orgonon, he bought a small organ on which he played his own music. In the first summers in Maine he used to play the accordion as a substitute for his beloved piano. He was definitely an amateur composer and musician, but as with all his attempts at different arts, I believe he might have achieved great things had he concentrated on one as a profession. He often daydreamed of being a great conductor. He was a strong admirer of Bruno Walter.

Coming back to the Vienna days: According to fellow students at the medical faculty in Vienna at that time, Annie Pink was one of the most attractive, brilliant, and sought after of the girls at the university. It was only to be expected that Reich, one of the most outstanding students, should win out over his competitors. He married Annie in 1921. Both continued their medical studies. Reich had started to earn a fairly good livelihood with psychoanalytic practice, and Annie's father helped with her studies. She, too, became a psychoanalyst, and could not help being drawn by Reich into the socialist movement of the twenties. With Reich, then and always, no personal relationship was possible unless one shared his professional and social interests and convictions.

The very active student groups at the university and the highly charged political atmosphere of Europe at that time could not fail to open new and exciting horizons to Reich. However, in the years between 1920 and 1924 the problems of psychoanalytic theory and practice were the most burning ones for him, and his interest in bioenergetics stayed in the foreground.

Reich always maintained that a red thread of logic led him from one step to the next. There was nothing astonishing in the fact that it crossed the lines of the various academic disciplines, because his main concept, always, from the very beginning, was the energy concept.

As I understood it, he was fascinated by Freud's libido theory and searched for the biological foundation of this theoretical concept of the sexual drives. This search led him to the discovery of bioenergetic functions, to the development of the orgasm theory, to the discovery of what he termed life energy or orgone energy which he then pursued in its various manifestations, all through his life, in human beings in their psyche and in their soma, in nature, in the atmosphere, and, eventually, in outer space. He spoke of our living in a vast ocean of orgone energy from which all living nature draws its sustaining energy.

Reich, with his great enthusiasm and capacity for work, was

a valuable asset to the Vienna Psychoanalytic Society. His first contribution, for a meeting on December 14, 1921, was a paper on an hysterical conversion symptom complex ("Konversionshysterischer Symptomenkomplex"). I don't remember whether it was on the occasion of this first contribution that Freud advised Reich never again to *read* a paper. He compared a lecturer reading his paper to a train engineer driving his locomotive at great speed while the passengers are running along, trying to catch up with it. Reich followed Freud's advice faithfully and I believe that he never again read a paper, though he was always well prepared for any talk or seminar.

From that time on, Reich was a regular contributor both to the meetings of the Psychoanalytic Society and to the *Internationale Zeitschrift für Psychoanalyse* (International Journal of Psychoanalysis). His first major paper on his main theme, however, was published in the *Zeitschrift für Sexualwissenschaft* (Journal of Sexology), and was entitled "Zur Triebenergetik" (About the Energetics of Drives), in 1923.

Despite Reich's preoccupation with scientific issues, the very exciting political atmosphere of these times could not fail to have its impact on him. The influence of the Russian revolution on the very active Austrian socialists, the many brilliant intellectuals who everywhere wrote about and discussed Marxism, could not leave the active and searching mind of Reich untouched. He started, with his usual thoroughness, to study Marx and Marxian philosophy. He joined the Austrian Socialist Party.

Reich's work in Freud's Psychoanalytic Polyclinic in the twenties brought him in closer contact with the working-class population, and he began at that time, in 1924, his studies into the social causation of mental illness. These studies led him to his attempts to reconcile Marxian and Freudian concepts, attempts that were eventually repudiated by both Marxists and Freudians. In his usual enthusiasm, he made some rather rash and naïve assumptions regarding the mental and sexual health of the proletariat which he later had to rectify.

Freud had established the Psychoanalytic Polyclinic in Vienna in 1922, and Reich had become first clinical assistant, a position he held until 1928 when he became its vice-director. He remained vice-director until 1930, when he left Vienna. During the same period, between 1924 and 1930, Reich was the director of the Seminar for Psychoanalytic Therapy, the training institute for psychoanalysts. Many American analysts who came to Vienna for training were not only attending Reich's seminars, but according to the psychoanalyst Dr. Walter Briehl (*Psychoanalytic Pioneers*, 1966), had been advised by their American training analysts and by Ferenczi to go to Reich for their personal analyses.

Reich himself underwent his first personal analysis with Dr. Isidore Sadger. This analysis was broken off by Reich unfinished, as were the following ones. The reason for the failure of all of Reich's attempts at a personal analysis will have to be discovered at some future date, if at all, by a person trained in the field of depth psychology.

Reich's main contributions to psychoanalytic theory and practice in the twenties were, first, the development of his orgasm theory, starting with his article "Ueber Genitalität" (About Genitality) in 1923, and continuing with lectures and seminars on the orgasm theory through 1926. This theory, to Reich's mind, laid the biological, scientific foundation for psychoanalytic theory. His second contribution was in the field of psychoanalytic practice. In developing character analysis, Reich moved farther and farther away from the passive role of the therapist as interpreter of material offered by the patient, to the more active therapy of including the patient's character, his characterologically based way of reacting, his whole behavior, including the muscular expressions and posture—what Reich later called the "muscular armoring" of his patient. The first paper on these new, active concepts of psychoanalytic practice was published in the *Internationale Zeitschrift für Psychoanalyse* in 1928, under the title "Ueber Charakteranalyse" (About Character Analysis). It was a forerunner of the book *Charakter Analyse*, published in 1933.

Analysts who attended Reich's seminar in Vienna in those years remember it as one of the most provocative and exciting parts of their training. Reich's vitality and enthusiasm carried the whole group; nobody could escape his influence. For many psychoanalysts, character analysis as presented at that time became an integral part of their work.

Among his many talents was Reich's ability to act. He told of how he would imitate various kinds of mental illnesses, or typical neurotic facial expressions and body postures, in order to get the point across to his students, and he always succeeded in it.

His family life at that time became more settled. His first child Eva was born in 1924, and he moved with his family into a larger apartment which he equipped, according to friends, with very fine and elegant furniture, all in good taste. As Annie Reich recalls it, the life they led was on the whole not very different from that of their friends and colleagues with whom they maintained a great deal of professional and social intercourse.

Earlier I talked about the contradictions in Reich's make-up, and it is here—while discussing Reich's personal circumstances—that one such contradiction comes to mind concerning his attitude toward money.

Reich could be generous to a fault. He liked to give good things when he felt like it, and he liked good things around him—the best and most tasteful in clothing, furnishings, and of course in tools and instruments. But he could be an absolute miser when it came to ordinary expenses for living. While he would readily spend much money on the apartment, he would become angry when it came, for example, to buying winter coats for the family. Reich's first wife Annie recalls that her father had to help finance her studies and frequently had to help with other expenses. I too remember scenes, much later, about the very modest amount Reich was willing to contribute toward his daughter Eva's medical education. Friends were always amazed at the very small allowance Reich gave me for running the household—an allowance which I always had to supplement from my own salary in order to make ends meet and, after our separation, to provide for our son Peter's upkeep. Reich would adamantly refuse to add ten dollars to the weekly household budget, and yet would give me as a birthday gift, a week later, a terribly expensive, very elegant leather suitcase which I really did not need. We once had quite a fight when I asked him for an extra eleven dollars to buy a pressure cooker to ease my household chores, while that same week he spent two thousand dollars on a microscope. His attitude toward money came up frequently in the course of my interviews with friends and co-workers, and played a definite part, even if a minor one, in his relations with others and myself.

His attitude toward money was among the reasons why he broke totally with his relatives in Vienna shortly after his return from the army. He blamed them for not providing adequately for his brother, so that the latter developed tuberculosis which eventually led to his early death. The brother had gone to live with maternal relatives in Roumania and married there at a very young age. He returned to Vienna with his wife and baby in 1925, desperately ill and poor. According to one informant, Reich supported his brother at that time and saw to it that he received good medical care. Another source told me that he not only did not provide for his brother, but absolutely refused to help his brother's widow and child in any way. There may be some truth in both these accounts, for in the area of money Reich was unpredictable. It seems, though, that he did help, together with other relatives, to support his brother and his brother's wife and child during the brother's illness and until his death in 1926; but only very occasionally would he assist the widow later on. Eventually he lost all contact with her.

His reasoning about monetary assistance in the late twenties was very much influenced by his militant socialism. Everybody had to work to support himself. Bourgeois parasitism was despicable to him. In 1929, after the big financial crash, he was approached by members of the family and asked for a rather modest monthly contribution toward the maintenance of his grandmother; she had lost her total income from dividends on which she had been able to live very well until then. He is reported to have refused any help with the justification that grandmother had never worked in all her life, only lived on the work of others, so let her go to the poorhouse now. He would, on the other hand, gladly help support the old cook Sosha, if she should need help.

Reich enjoyed his daughter Eva and there is no doubt that that his first-born child was always his favorite. The concept of self-regulation which later on played such an important role in his work had not yet appeared, and the infant was brought up on a very rigid feeding schedule, a fact which Reich later on deplored.

In Reich's early activities in the psychoanalytic movement, Freud had regarded him as one of his most brilliant assistants. Reich was a "favorite son" and had free access to Freud's house; he could go there to discuss problems with Freud whenever the need arose. Freud then regarded Reich's insistence on the sexual basis for every neurosis as Reich's *Steckenpferd* (hobby-horse), and he described it as such in one of his letters to Lou Andreas-Salomé.

Reich himself never lost his admiration for Freud's achievements, even after his later separation from psychoanalysis. He always stressed his indebtedness to Freud's life work, and his personal attachment to Freud himself lasted throughout his life, even after Freud's later rejection of him. One of Reich's treasured possessions, in his library to this day, was a photograph of Freud with a personal inscription: "Herrn Dr. Wilh. Reich zur freundlichen Erinnerung an Sigm. Freud. März 1925" (Dr. Wilh. Reich in friendly remembrance of Sigm. Freud. March 1925).

Early in 1927, Reich came into a severe conflict with Freud. It is difficult to come to definite conclusions about this major event. Friends, foes, family, Freud biographers, Reich's own account—all give different interpretations.

Some maintain that it was Reich's political involvement, his attempts at a Marxian interpretation of psychoanalysis, which brought on the 1927 conflict—although Reich's full involvement with political movements did not come until 1928. Others seem to think that it was Reich's stress on the sexual basis for every neurosis that became more and more uncomfortable to Freud. Annie Reich holds that it was the refusal of Freud to take Reich for personal analysis that lead to the serious break; at first it had seemed possible that Freud would accept him, but Freud later decided he could or would not break the rule he had made not to accept anyone of his Viennese circle for personal analysis. Reich himself attributed the break to theoretical differences, mainly regarding the social implications of psychoanalysis, and to attempts by other analysts, among them Dr. Paul Federn, to discredit him with Freud out of professional jealousy.

There seems to be little doubt that there was an attempt on the part of some Viennese analysts to undermine Reich's theoretical influence on the younger generation of analysts. And there is no doubt that the theoretical differences between Freud and Reich grew sharper. But on the basis of my personal understanding of Reich, and the observations I have been able to make about his reactions in somewhat similar situations, I would tend to accept Annie Reich's version of the conflict. Freud had become, as I see it in simple terms, a father substitute for Reich. The rejection, as Reich felt it, was intolerable. Reich reacted to this rejection with deep depression.

At nearly the same time, Reich developed tuberculosis of the lungs—whether psychosomatically connected with his upset or not, we don't know—and had to spend several months in a sanitarium in Davos, Switzerland. Reich's father and brother had died from this illness.

Reich did not spend the months in Davos in idleness. He wrote several reviews and articles for the *Internationale Zeitschrift für Psychoanalyse,* and kept in touch with the work done in the Clinic and Seminar. He finished his book *Die Funktion des Orgasmus* (The Function of the Orgasm) which was published in 1927 by International Psychoanalytic Publishing House. Briefly, and in very elementary terms, I shall try to give the main points of this very important step in the development of Reich's work on the energy concept and its function in the human body. Reich's theories hold that sexual energy is being built up in the body and needs release through orgasm, involving the total body. If the natural release of the energy is inhibited for one reason or another, stasis of the energy sets in, giving rise to all kinds of neurotic mechanisms. Release of the dammed-up energy through re-establishment of the function of the orgasm is the therapeutic goal, since it would establish the natural flow of energy and eliminate the neurosis.

Annie Reich, and with her other Freudian analysts, believe that a "deteriorating process" began in Reich during his stay at the sanitarium, that he was not the same person after his return, that he must have gained new insights into some of his own problems and been disturbed by them. This theory has been advanced again and again by those attacking theories developed by Reich at this time and later. I feel that this is a mistaken viewpoint in general and on the part of Annie Reich specifically a rationalization of her personal difficulties in living with Reich because he was an unusual person with unusual energy. Reich had a driving force that made it very hard for anyone to follow him, or to live with him for any length of time. He was violent of temperament, taxing people around him to the utmost, but he was at the same time terribly exciting to be with, and it was a privilege to participate in his enthusiasm and to share his insights.

I met Reich in 1939, and until 1951 our life together, although not always running smoothly, did not make me feel that a "deteriorating process" was going on. He had gone through real and incredible persecutions by that time. He had been expelled by the

International Psychoanalytic Association; he had many times been driven to emigrations by colleagues to whom he had become embarrassing through his political affiliations, or by political organizations to whom he had become embarrassing through his work on sexuality; he had endured the unpleasant Norwegian newspaper campaign—all of these happenings I shall try to describe extensively in context. During these years Reich was suspicious of many people—often with good reason—but he managed to gather a group of serious and well-trained physicians and psychologists around him in Scandinavia, and again in the United States, to build up organizations which functioned well, and to continue his work with undiminished vigor and strength.

I have talked to many of his former friends, colleagues, and co-workers in Scandinavia. Some of them have separated themselves from Reich's later work in orgonomy; some may have a quarrel with certain aspects of his psychotherapy; some may have been disappointed by his reactions to them personally—but every single one of them recognized the greatness of the man, and not one of them doubted his sanity in these years. If he showed any delusions of grandeur, or paranoid tendencies, he was the first to see them and to ridicule them. And if he did develop such tendencies after a severe heart attack in 1951, and after renewed, very real attacks on his work became stronger and more vicious, that does not detract one iota from his achievements. One must evaluate Reich's scientific theories and contributions scientifically.

Reich returned to Vienna early in the summer of 1927, quickly recovered from his bout with tuberculosis. With his old vitality and energy, he took up his functions and his practice again. At this point his political life became most active. After his disappointment with the Austrian Social Democrats in what he considered their sellout to party bosses in 1927, he joined the Communist Party in 1928. Despite the demands on his time by his work in the Polyclinic, his training seminar, his flourishing private practice, and his theoretical work, he became a very active member. He participated in demonstrations, helped in the distributions of leaflets, and spoke at meetings and to youth groups, mostly on problems of mental hygiene. In his book *People in Trouble* he writes about his incredible naïveté then in believing in the strength of revolutionary dedication to overcome political adversaries. He speaks about the reasons for his very active participation, his need to understand the working-class population, and the reaction of the masses to political situations and pressures. In that book he sees himself in retrospect, as a nonpolitical participant acting solely as the physician interested in the mental hygiene problems of the proletariat. He maintained all through his later years that he was never a political worker. It is true, he never accepted a political office, but it is also obvious if one reads the account of his activities, and if one talks to people associated with him during those years, that he definitely was politically involved although his activities were mainly in the mental hygiene field of these movements and organizations.

Reich realized before many of his contemporaries the crying need for mental health centers. With four psychoanalytic colleagues and three obstetricians he founded the Sozialistische Gesellschaft für Sexualberatung und Sexualforschung (Socialist Society for Sex Consultation and Sexological Research). In January 1929 they opened the first sex hygiene clinics for workers and employees (Sexualberatungs-Klinik für Arbeiter und Angestellte), which gave free information on birth control, child rearing, sex education for children and adolescents, and were open to the public for lectures and discussions. Reich devoted himself to these clinics for two years, until 1930, when he decided to leave Vienna to go to Berlin where he had made arrangements for a personal analysis with Dr. Sandor Rado.

In 1928 Reich's second daughter Lore was born. Reich and his wife were active in the psychoanalytic organization, and their social life, as mentioned before, revolved mostly around other colleagues and their families. Annie participated to a certain extent in his political activities, but my guess would be—as explained earlier—that it was more because of the impossibility of sharing Reich's life without sharing his interests to the last than out of her own involvement with these problems. Summer vacations were spent in the Austrian Alps with the children and with friends. Reich enjoyed mountain climbing, and there are photos in the Reich archives of the children with their parents, and of Reich as a proud conqueror of alpine peaks.

During 1928–1930 Reich's efforts were largely directed toward a reconciliation between Marxist theory and psychoanalysis, efforts which culminated in *Dialektischer Materialismus und Psychoanalyse* (Dialectic Materialism and Psychoanalysis), first published in a Moscow periodical *Pod Swaminjen Marxisma,* No. 718, 1929. An excerpt appeared in the *Almanach der Psychoanalyse,* 1930, in Vienna, under the title "Die Dialektik im Seelischen" (Dialectics and Psychology). The book was eventually reprinted again in 1934 by Sexpol-Verlag in Denmark.

Two short pamphlets, written more or less for the people who came to the sex hygiene clinics, and based on Reich's experiences and observations in these clinics, were published between 1929 and 1930 by Münsterverlag in Vienna. They were entitled, respectively, *Sexualerregung und Sexualbefriedigung* (Sexual Excitation and Sexual Satisfaction) and *Geschlechtsreife, Enthaltsamkeit, Ehemoral* (Sexual Maturity, Abstinence, Marital Morality). The latter was included in the book *Die Sexualität im Kulturkampf* (The Sexual Revolution) published later, in 1936. These treatises were written from the point of view of a militant communist, very critical of the bourgeois morality and its laws; but apart from the political bias, they contained sound insights into the problems of mental hygiene and the sexual attitudes of the population in general.

The exciting developments in the mental hygiene field in the Soviet Union between 1917 and 1927, such as the liberalization of laws concerning marriage, divorce, abortion, homosexuality, birth control, the new insights into child development, child upbringing, juvenile delinquency, the experiments in education that were reported at international congresses and in publications by such educators as Vera Schmidt, aroused Reich's curiosity to go and see for himself what was happening in that country. He arranged with some Russian colleagues for a lecture tour and the opportunity to observe some of the experimental child-care centers and nurseries. He left for Moscow in September 1929 for a brief tour. He gave one lecture on "Sociology and Psychology" at the Communist Academy in Moscow, and another one on "Prevention of Neuroses" at the Neuropsychiatric Institute. He met with Vera Schmidt and other teachers for long discussions, and visited a number of the kindergartens and child-care centers. But he did not find the full understanding of his concepts that he had expected. Although impressed with some of the physical aspects of some of the centers, he felt that many of the physicians and educators whom he observed and with whom he talked had the same "bourgeois," moralistic attitudes about childhood sexuality as their colleagues in the capitalist countries. He wrote about his disappointment, after all or most of the liberalized laws had been rescinded in the Soviet Union, in the second part of the 1945 edition of *The Sexual Revolution,* under the title "The Struggle for the 'New Life' in the Soviet Union."

After his return from Russia, he spent one more year in Vienna in private practice and was deeply involved in both the psychoanalytic movement and in political activities in connection with the mental hygiene centers. He moved to Berlin in the fall of 1930.

Berlin: 1930–1933

Reich's political activities became more and more uncomfortable to the Vienna Psychoanalytic Society and led, of necessity, to further personal conflicts. Reich felt a growing need for a personal analysis, and on the advice of Freud and several colleagues he decided to go to Berlin where the psychoanalyst Rado had consented to accept him for analysis. Reich moved to Berlin at the end of September 1930.

Annie Reich is critical of Rado for accepting Reich, because at the time he made his arrangement with Reich he knew he was going to the United States within six months. He left Reich, as she sees it, in the midst of a depression, his analysis unfinished. She feels that this contributed further to Reich's "deteriorating process."

Again, it seems strange that while she talks about his "deep depression" and "deterioration" he was, according to others, full of his usual energy, an active participant in the Berlin Psychoanalytic Society, and an effective force in the Communist Party. Several of the German psychoanalysts of the time, among them Erich Fromm and Siegfried Bernfeld, were Marxist in outlook. In his numerous discussions with them and others, Reich received their serious attention and comprehension when he expounded his theory of integrating Marx and psychoanalysis. This theory had grown from Reich's belief that every psychotherapist had an obligation to cure not only the problems of the individual patient, but the problems of society as a whole. It was not enough to treat mental illness; one had to learn its social causation, and even more important, its prophylaxis.

Dr. Otto Fenichel, the psychoanalyst who had belonged to the professional and social circle around the Reichs in Vienna, and who had himself moved to Berlin, often joined in the discussions; he, together with Reich, started to organize some of the young German psychoanalysts into a group of dialectic-materialistic psychoanalysts.

In November 1930 Reich gave a well-received lecture on the prevention of neuroses to the Berlin Association of Socialist Physicians. The soil for politically oriented physical and psychiatric medicine was certainly more fertile in Berlin than in Vienna at that time. He gave a series of lecture courses at the Marxistische Arbeiter Schule (MASCH), a socialist adult-education center. Although I did not know Reich at that time, I still remember an enthusiastic account of these particular lectures which one of his listeners, a young worker and student at the MASCH, gave to a group of fellow emigrants in Paris, in 1934.

Reich's involvement with the politically oriented mental hygiene movement became more or less the dominant factor in his life in Berlin. The German Communist Party agreed to the organization of an association on the basis of Reich's sex-political platform, the Deutscher Reichsverband für Proletarische Sexualpolitik (German Association for Proletarian Sexual Politics) which had a membership of more than 20,000. The platform contained the following demands as its main points:

a) better housing conditions for the masses of people;
b) abolition of laws against abortion and homosexuality;
c) change of marriage and divorce laws;
d) free birth-control advice and contraceptives;
e) health protection of mothers and children;
f) nurseries in factories and in other large employment centers;
g) abolition of laws prohibiting sex education;
h) home leave for prisoners.

Reich traveled a great deal all over Germany, giving lectures and helping to establish hygiene centers in key industrial cities under the auspices of the Reichsverband.

The rise of fascism, and the reaction of the masses of people to it, became an important part of his theoretical work, culminating in *Die Massenpsychologie des Faschismus,* published in 1933 (English edition, *The Mass Psychology of Fascism,* 1946). Although this book was written under the impact of the experience of German fascism, its mass-psychological insights are applicable to totalitarian society in general. It has been, next to *Character Analysis,* Reich's most widely read and acclaimed book.

In 1931 Reich and some colleagues established the Verlag für Sexualpolitik (Sexpol-Verlag) in Berlin. They published immediately some pamphlets on sex education for children, *Wenn Dein Kind Dich Fragt* (When Your Child Asks Questions); for "proletarian" youth there was *Der Sexuelle Kampf der Jugend* (The Sexual Struggle of Youth), a booklet which Reich later repudiated because of its politically biased orientation. Reich extended his criticism of bourgeois sexual mores, using Malinowski's anthropological studies of the Trobriand Islanders, *The Sexual Life of The Savages,* as a basis. Reich tried to give a theoretical explanation of the development of mankind from matriarchal to patriarchal to authoritarian society. His thesis, briefly, states that based on economically determined sexual taboos, sexual repression leads eventually to submissiveness to authoritarian family and authoritarian state, the breeding places of mental illness and totalitarianism. These studies were published in book form by Sexpol-Verlag in 1932, under the title *Der Einbruch der Sexualmoral.* (These studies have not been published in English. The title, roughly, means the development or breaking through or breaking in of sexual morality.) Since Malinowski's approach differed from that of the anthropologist G. Roheim whose studies were considered by most analysts of that time to support orthodox psychoanalysis, heated discussions provoked by Reich's book developed between the two schools.

Reich did not neglect theoretical and practical psychoanalytic work during this time. Although not permitted to act as a training analyst in the Berlin Psychoanalytic Society because of his insistence on character-analytic therapy, he was nevertheless working within the framework of the society as a lecturer, mainly on aspects of character analysis. His book, *Die Charakteranalyse,* originally slated for publication by Internationale Psychoanalytischer Verlag, was later rejected by them and was published by Sexpol-Verlag in Berlin in 1933.

Against the advice of Rado, Annie Reich and the children followed Reich to Berlin. Reich's identification with the proletarian movement was so great at that time that he put before his wife the alternative of either placing the children in a communist children's center or agreeing to a separation. Annie consented to the children being sent to the home, although she feels today that this was a great mistake on her part. The children recall the home as a very unhappy experience. It was not easy for them to obey the demands made on them to be good little communists. Annie remembers an incident when two-year-old Lore received a stern lecture from her father for singing: "Oh, Tannenbaum . . ." instead of a good revolutionary, proletarian song.

Reich's active support of the mental hygiene clinics operated by the Reichsverband, and their constantly increasing membership between 1931 and 1932, encountered mounting opposition from political functionaries of the German Communist Party. They feared that diverting interest to mental hygiene problems would weaken the revolutionary ardor for the party, especially among the youth groups. Eventually, even before the defeat of the communists by Hitler, the party repudiated Reich, ordered the withdrawal of his literature from its bookstores, and prohibited the sale and distribution of his books and pamphlets within its organizations. According to Reich's description of these events, there was some opposition among the rank and file against this order which had come from the high political functionaries.

Just as the psychoanalysts found Reich's political involvement at this time of political turmoil highly compromising and began their efforts to exclude him from the International Psychoanalytic Association, so did the communists find Reich's insistence on sexual politics too compromising to tolerate, and he was officially excluded from the party in 1933.

No one with any political sense living in Germany during that period could escape the feeling of imminent catastrophe. But still people hoped, and went on with their efforts to stem the mounting fascist tide. Reich, with his usual optimism, worked for his objectives against all odds until the day Hitler seized power.

Already in those days, as always later on, when he was totally immersed in an idea, a movement, a theory, only the absolutes were possible for Reich. Something was either black or white, you were for him or against him, never a compromise, never a shade of gray permissible. And those close to him had to follow him or get out—regardless of whether they could or were able to understand what it was all about. I think, theoretically, he expected people to know what they were doing, to follow him in his pursuits because they knew he was right or that his theories were correct or because they felt about these things the same way he did. But in practice he overlooked the fact that few of those around him were equipped, emotionally or otherwise, to follow him or to understand his theories. They would follow, if they did, out of admiration, out of love, out of blind loyalty or, sometimes, out of fear of being kicked out of his orbit. The power of his personality was enormous, and was difficult to withstand. It was this inflexible attitude of his, more than anything else, that again and again lost him friends and co-workers.

Reich's family life had by this time almost disintegrated. The children had been sent to their maternal grandparents in Vienna. Annie was still in Berlin, but it had become clear to both her and Reich that their relationship was no longer tenable. The differences in their professional attitudes toward psychoanalysis and the Psychoanalytic Association, in their political involvements, in their views on the upbringing of the children became wider—and with the widening gap, given Reich's character, the personal relationship had to break. They left Germany together in the first days of March 1933, and as they had Austrian passports, encountered no difficulties in reaching Vienna. Their final separation came at that time.

Scandinavia: 1933-1939

Upon his return to Vienna, Reich found a very unpromising -climate for his activities. Old professional connections were broken and difficult to re-establish. In political circles, there was as yet little understanding of the far reaching consequences of the events in Germany.

At the occasion of various congresses of the World League for Sexual Reform, especially at the Congress in 1930 where he read an important paper, Reich had established close connections with one of the league's directors, Dr. J. H. Leunbach of Copenhagen. Upon the urging of Dr. Leunbach and a young Danish analyst who had come to Reich for training in Berlin, Reich decided to transfer his activities to Denmark. He was at that time still working within the Psychoanalytic Association, and now he asked for official permission to work for the association as a teaching and training analyst in Denmark. It took the association a long time to decide; eventually, permission was refused because of Reich's political affiliations and his therapeutic deviation from orthodox analysis. However, Reich had already started to work in that capacity with Danish analysts and with some German emigrant physicians who had followed him. He also worked hard at finishing the manuscript of the *Massenpsychologie des Faschismus* which he felt needed to be published most urgently. Sexpol-Verlag was transferred to Copenhagen, and it was possible with much personal financial sacrifice of his own and on the part of his co-workers and students to publish this book in August 1933.

In his book *People in Trouble,* Reich tells how in these early days of the emigration in Denmark the communist organization Rote Hilfe (Red Help), established for the specific purpose of helping emigrants, treated people who had barely escaped with their lives in an unbelievably high-handed, bureaucratic way. This was for him the last straw, and he broke then and there with the party, even before his official expulsion.

Reich detested all political bureaucracy. It was to him the ultimate misuse of formal authority. His experience with communist bureaucracy was the starting point for his attacks against communism which made him, later on, an almost obsessional foe of Stalinism, red fascism, and all forms of totalitarianism. This, however, did not keep him from always recognizing the debt he owed Marxian philosophy and theory in the development of his own work-democratic concepts, to be explained later.

During the 1932 May Day demonstration in Berlin, Reich had met Elsa Lindenberg who was a member of the cell to which he belonged and which numbered among its members Arthur Koestler and other prominent writers and artists. Elsa, a dancer with the ballet of the Berliner Staatsoper, was a dedicated, courageous political worker. She remained in Berlin after Hitler's seizure of power as a political underground worker until the danger became such that she had to leave to save her life. She joined Reich in Denmark, where she began studies that influenced her work as therapist in body movement and as teacher in contemporary dance, using the principles of Reich's theory of muscular armoring. Later, in Norway, she was engaged as a choreographer at the National Theater in Oslo. Elsa Lindenberg became Reich's second wife, and although the relationship never was legalized, it was a binding, marital relationship to their eyes and to the eyes of the world.

Reich had worked for about six months in Denmark when the Danish government revoked his permit of sojourn. In his *People in Trouble* he blames this on the leftist politicians in Denmark, the psychiatrists, and the Psychoanalytic Association. Freud had officially declared his disagreement with Reich's theoretical principles and therefore did not think him suited to be a teaching analyst; this added to Reich's difficulties in settling permanently in Denmark. Reich had to decide once again where to take his work, where he would find the most receptive soil for his theories. For these and other reasons, he started on a European tour.

He first went to England where he met with a group of analysts at the home of the British analyst Dr. Ernest Jones. He found the atmosphere personally friendly, but little receptive to his theoretical work. His identification with Malinowski's anthropological work, among other things, was contrary to Jones's interpretation of anthropology, and the English analysts feared the intrusion of a politically compromising analyst who was developing, at the same time, a new approach to therapy with emphasis on the sexual basis of neuroses. They certainly did not encourage Reich to bring his work to England and to settle there.

It is interesting to note here that after the later difficulties in the United States in 1956–1957, and after Reich's death, A. S. Neill of Summerhill School and others seemed to feel that Reich would never have encountered these difficulties if he had decided to settle in England at that time.

One very pleasurable aspect of his sojourn in England was Reich's meeting with Malinowski. They enjoyed each other's company and soon became such good friends that they decided to call each other *du*. To a non-German-speaking person this may not appear as something special, but in the German-speaking, academic, nonsocialist world, this is a sign of close friendship and intimate understanding. Their mutual appreciation and feeling of friendship continued when they both were lecturing at the New School for Social Research in New York in 1940–1941.

Reich decided that London as a place to settle was out. Paris and Zürich, which he briefly visited, he never even considered.

After a short stay in the Austrian Alps with his children, whom he had not seen for seven months, he decided to follow the advice of his Scandinavian students and settle in Malmö, Sweden. He returned to Denmark, passing through Czechoslovakia and Germany. In Austria the innumerable factions of the socialist movement were busily arguing about minute differences in their interpretations of Marxian theory, and wishful thinking about an immediately impending uprising of the socialist masses to crush fascism was still in full bloom; it was risky for Reich to travel through Czechoslovakia and Germany, but after his visit to Austria he wished to get a personal impression of life under Hitler. He left Germany, after a brief stopover in Berlin, with the feeling that there was a fast-growing militarism in the atmosphere. He felt that despite the heroic efforts of the underground workers of which he had heard and read, and despite the wishful dreams of the emigrants, the masses of the people were sluggish, taking the easy way out by "following the Führer." He put these ideas and experiences into a short treatise which appeared under the title "Was ist Klassenbewusstsein?" (What is Class Consciousness?) under the pseudonym of Ernst Parell. It was published in the newly established *Zeitschrift für Politische Psychologie und Sexualökonomie* (Journal for Political Psychology and Sex-Economy) by Sexpol-Verlag in Copenhagen in 1934. The use of the pseudonym served two purposes, as I see it. First, it would not give away the fact that Reich had traveled through Germany in case he wanted to return again, and second, it separated the scientist Reich from the political man Parell. Also, I think that Reich enjoyed the feeling of secrecy in the use of pseudonyms. Much later, in 1955 and 1956, he lived in Washington, D.C. under another one of his pseudonyms, Walter Roner, when there was really no need for it.

We have encountered the term *Sexual-Politik* (sex politics) before. This term is based on the concept that human society with its laws is directed not only by demands of an economic and materialistic nature, but even more by the conscious and unconscious demands of sexual drives and their use or misuse in political, public life. We now find the term sex-economy included in the title of the newly established journal *Zeitschrift für Politische Psychologie und Sexualökonmie,* and later in the name of the International Institute for Sex-Economy which Reich founded in Norway in 1936.

An extensive explanation of the concept and theory of sex-economy may be found in an article by Reich's friend and co-worker, the Norwegian psychologist Dr. Ola Raknes, in the *International Journal of Sex-Economy and Orgone Research,* 1944, under the pseudonym of Carl Arnold. (The reason for the publication of this and other articles under pseudonyms was to protect Scandinavian colleagues from repercussions during the war situation.) Dr. Raknes gives the translation of the words from their Greek and Latin origins as meaning the teaching and study of the use of sexual energy. The concept of sex-economy is an extension of the orgasm theory to include not only the character formation and neurotic stasis mechanisms, but body musculature, the role of muscular tensions, and the role of the autonomous nervous system. In short, it means the way in which the body handles its sexual, i.e. life, energy in both the psychological and the somatic realm.

In September 1933 Reich settled in Malmö. It was easily reached by boat from Copenhagen, so that those of his trainees who wanted to continue their studies with him could come over every other day. Elsa, who was to finish her work in Copenhagen, would come for the weekends.

The group in Denmark, with most of whose members he kept in close touch during his entire stay in Scandinavia, and many of whom came to Oslo later for further study, included besides Dr. Leunbach also Dr. Lotte Liebeck, a member of the Berlin Marxist psychoanalytic group. She was in the early thirties a good friend and co-worker of Reich, interested especially in his character-analytic approach to psychotherapy, and working with him on its elaboration. Among others was a young psychoanalyst, Dr. Tage Philipson. Both Dr. Leunbach and Dr. Philipson were very active in birth-control clinics, and advocated a change in the abortion laws—and because of that were in difficulties with the Danish authorities. Also in the group were several teachers, especially nursery and kindergarten teachers with good training in psychology. They worked with the concept of self-regulation, and many of their interesting observations were later published in the *Zeitschrift.* Reich's relationship with these co-workers and students was informal and friendly. Since many of them were socialists, the informal *du* and first names were quite frequent. Only the academicians among the group kept to the formal ways of address.

In June 1934 Reich's permit to live and work in Sweden was revoked. Several influential people among Reich's friends tried to intervene with the Swedish authorities to have Reich's permit of sojourn made permanent, but without success. The sex-political and psychoanalytic training activities were not really understood, and just because of that gave the impression that something subversive was going on; the combination of sex, psychoanalysis, and politics was too much for the authorities to absorb. Again, Reich had to leave. His friends persuaded him to spend his summer holidays in a country home on the coast of Denmark, illegally and under an assumed name. The children came to spend the summer with him, and despite the adversities they seem to have had a good vacation together.

Elsa recalls that Eva idolized her father and identified strongly with him. Reich enjoyed the children and liked to play and swim with them. Reich's ideas on child upbringing had developed together with his other theories in the direction of self-regulation, self-expression, and freedom. But he was very annoyed when on their trip together back to Switzerland at the end of their vacation, the children showed poor manners in the first-class dining room on the ship; and he was angry at their provoking the other passengers to call them "circus people" by showing off some acrobatic tricks. This sounds very familiar to me because later, with our son Peter, Reich always insisted with great strictness on good behavior and proper table manners in public places. On the whole, however, this summer on the coast seems to have been an enjoyable and peaceful period before another very painful event which followed at the 13th International Psychoanalytic Congress in Lucerne, Switzerland, at the end of August 1934.

Several times previous to this congress, before and during 1933, the German Psychoanalytic Society had asked Reich to resign because his name on the membership list had become a heavy burden under the growing fascist influence. Each time, Reich had refused to resign because he felt that his scientific contributions to the body of psychoanalytic knowledge far outweighed the danger that his political affiliations would mean to the association. Shortly before the congress started, he was informed by the secretary of the German Society that his name had been omitted from the membership list because of the political situation, but that this would not affect his standing in the International Psychoanalytic Association because it was planned at the congress to recognize the Scandinavian group in which Reich was assured membership. Reich protested about this action to Freud's daughter Anna, the general secretary of the association, who disclaimed any knowledge of the matter and referred it to Dr. Ernest Jones of the executive committee. It soon became apparent that the executive committee wanted to make the recognition of the Scandinavians dependent on the condition that they would not accept Reich as a member. The Norwegian group, however, mainly Ola Raknes, Nic (Hoel) Waal, and Harald Schjelderup refused to accept a conditional recognition, and in the end were unconditionally accepted. But they were separated officially from the Swedish group in order to keep the latter out of Reich's influence.

It has to be stressed that Reich, contrary to many other interpretations of this event, had very definitely been in effect *expelled* from the International Psychoanalytic Association. He would not voluntarily have resigned under any kind of pressure, and he had stated so on many occasions.

The Norwegian group, of course, offered membership to Reich, but after long deliberation Reich decided to stay outside the psychoanalytic organizations entirely. He had to come to the conclusion that his work within the framework of psychoanalysis was coming to an end, and that the development of his theoretical work on bioenergetics was at variance with many of Freud's theories, among them the death-instinct theory. His practical, therapeutic approach, with its constantly expanding character-analytic technique, was likewise at variance with orthodox Freudian therapy. The dialectic-materialistic psychology which had been the nucleus of his work in Berlin with Fenichel, had developed into sex-economy.

Reich was scheduled to give a paper at the congress on "Psychischer Kontakt und Vegetative Strömung" (Psychological Contact and Vegetative Streamings) which he gave as a guest lecturer, and which has to be regarded as his first attempt at a unified psychosomatic concept.

Looking back at the events of 1934, painful as the now complete break from his long association with Freud and the psychoanalytic movement must have been for Reich, especially in the way it was handled, it was a logical and even necessary event. His work, one must recognize, had become an independent effort, growing out and away from the mother organization. He himself recognized that the body of knowledge which he had elaborated, though a logical continuation of psychoanalytic concepts, could no longer be reconciled with the now well established, generally recognized, main work of psychoanalysis. Psychoanalysis had finally become a respectable, and respected, and—let's not forget it—lucrative profession, and few were willing to venture into new and uncertain fields, exciting and promising as they were to those few who did follow Reich.

The break with the psychoanalytic organization meant a break with many old friends and associates, and the feeling of loneliness, of being without a home for his work, must have been very strong in Reich. A weaker person might have completely broken under the strain of such a loss, but Reich, with his unbelievable energy and optimism, bounced back and threw himself into the building up of his own, independent organization with the help of the few courageous and devoted people he had gained through this ordeal.

One of the old friends who had emigrated to Oslo, who supported Reich and wanted to follow him in his new venture, was Otto Fenichel. However, he later found the sex-economic developments more and more difficult to accept, and even came to feel his livelihood threatened by Reich. A growing number of the Scandinavian analysts preferred to go into training with Reich, to learn the new technique of character-analysis, and Fenichel found his practice dwindling. His friendship turned into hatred, according to many observers. In 1935, Fenichel left Scandinavia and went via Czechoslovakia and Switzerland to the United States. The rumor that could never be laid to rest all through the following years, namely that Reich had a breakdown and was completely mad, seems to be traceable to Otto Fenichel. When Dr. Theodore Wolfe traveled the same route a few years later on his way back to the States, telling colleagues in Czechoslovakia, Switzerland, and France that he came from working with Reich in Oslo, he encountered the same rumor over and over again. Fenichel was always mentioned as its source.

For Reich it was another loss of a friend and colleague with whom he had shared both work and leisure over a great many years. He was bitter about it, and could never quite understand why Fenichel reacted with so much hatred against him.

After the congress Reich and his wife made a short camping trip through Switzerland before returning to Denmark. Reich liked the informality of camping, the feeling of being close to nature, away from the noise and bustle of tourists in hotels. I remember a young relative of mine who had gone on a hiking trip to Switzerland that summer coming back to Paris and telling us proudly that he had been picked up as a hitchhiker by Reich and his wife, and that they had invited him to share their lunch. After the publication of *Mass Psychology* Reich had become something of a hero to young socialists.

In October 1934 Reich moved with his second wife and his belongings to Oslo. The children remained with their mother in Vienna.

Dr. Harald Schjelderup, the Director of the Psychological Institute of the University of Oslo, who had been in training with Reich in Denmark, invited him to give a series of lectures on Character Analysis and Biophysics at the institute. Some months later, the facilities of the institute were put at his disposal, enabling him to start his long-contemplated experiments on the bioelectric nature of sexuality and anxiety. For quite a while, Reich had thought that it should be possible to measure electrically the excitation of biological energy in the erogenous zones of the body; that through vagotonic and sympatheticotonic reactions as expressed, for instance, in the contraction and relaxation of muscles or the opening and closing of valves, it should be possible to show experimentally the antithesis of the pleasure and anxiety reactions found in the functions of the autonomous nervous system. The results of these experiments with an oscillograph were published by Sexpol-Verlag in 1937, under the title "Experimentelle Ergebnisse über die elektrische Funktion von Sexualität und Angst" (Experimental Results Regarding the Electrical Function of Sexuality and Anxiety). Many of Reich's co-workers, assistants, and students put themselves at his disposal and served as human guinea pigs for these experiments. The oscillograph, wired to the person, would record reactions to opposite stimuli, such as sugar or salt on the tongue, soft stroking or scratching of skin surfaces, and so on. There was no sexual intercourse between the participants.

There were quite a few scientists—and analysts—at that time who thought that Reich's experiments were "crazy," that they were "unrealistic." But looking at today's literature on experiments being conducted on various aspects of human sexual behavior, one can only conclude that Reich was some thirty years ahead in his ideas, and not so unrealistic or crazy at all.

There was a comparatively peaceful period of work between 1935 and 1937. In the summer of 1935 a sort of summer school developed, with courses and lectures. It was not at first a formal organization; friends, students, and assistants gathered in the Norwegian countryside, some camping, making it a *Zeltlager* (tenting ground), some living in nearby boarding houses, all studying and listening. The atmosphere was casual, in great contrast to the much more formal climate that was to prevail in the American organization later on. In my quest for information in Scandinavia, I was struck again and again by the way people referred to Reich as Willy. No one in America, except his closest family, and some of his old friends from Austria, ever referred to him as Willy. He was always Reich to a few, and Dr. Reich to most.

In the fall of 1935, a seminar for psychotherapy started, with Reich's own trainees and other psychotherapists. Dr. Ola Raknes remembers Reich as the most brilliant leader of this seminar, with an unfailing eye for the important points in the situations under discussion.

Among Reich's close friends in Oslo were some outstanding figures of Norwegian literature, among them Sigurd Hoel and the Poet Laureate of Norway Arnulf Oeverland. They used to meet regularly at the well-known Theater Café, opposite the National Theater, and they became known as habitués, everybody gasping and looking at them in awe when they entered. One can today see some of Oslo's well-known personalities of the theater and the arts having their regular meeting place at this café.

Reich wrote innumerable articles on both aspects of the *Zeitschrift,* i.e., on political psychology and on sex-economic developments between 1934 and 1939. Besides the lecture course at the Psychological Institute, he gave a few talks to student organizations, and at the Arbeidersamfund, a workers union. But his active participation in any political movement or organization had stopped by that time. Elsa, who was then occasionally doing the choreography for a "red revue" at the Arbeidersamfund, told how Reich came to a rehearsal once and insisted on helping with the drilling of a Prussian goosestep. She recalls also the warm, direct contact Reich had with these young workers, and how everybody enjoyed a big party after the revue was over. Reich insisted on writing verses for the next revue, but, according to Elsa, they were very banal in sentiment. As in his other attempts in the arts, his poetry was strictly amateurish but without doubt showed much talent.

During his stay in Oslo, Reich became a great admirer of the Norwegian painter Edvard Munch. His later efforts at painting show a very definite influence of Munch. Ola Raknes told me later that when he first saw Reich's paintings at Orgonon in the fifties he immediately recognized Munch's influence, and when I went to the Munch Museum in Oslo, not having been too well acquainted with Munch's oils, I was surprised at how much he had influenced Reich.

In February 1936 Reich together with a number of his Scandinavian friends and colleagues founded the Institut für Sexualökonomische Lebensforschung (Institute for Sex-Economic Bioresearch). A building was found where all aspects of the work could be brought together under one roof: the experimental laboratory work, the teaching and training courses, and publishing activities. The official language of the institute was German. Reich employed mainly German political refugees as secretaries, as laboratory assistants, and as staff for the publishing house, although there were some Norwegians working as assistants. Most of the better educated Norwegians were quite fluent in German before the World War II invasion, and still are today, although they are reluctant to speak it. Among those working with Reich at that time were physicians and psychologists, educators, nursery and kindergarten teachers, sociologists and artists, and laboratory assistants.

Some of the Germans, especially those who worked in the publishing house, ran into some difficulties with Reich. Since it was *his* effort and *his* organization on which things ran, he had to have the prerogative to make final decisions. But some of these young socialists insisted on a political way of running the publishing house with equal rights for everybody. When Reich, in his rather forceful way, insisted on his rights, he was called a dictator. These experiences helped Reich to formulate his concepts for a work-democratic organization as opposed to a political one. We shall hear more about the work-democratic theories later on.

In the training sessions with the therapists, and together with them, Reich continued the development of his character-analytic therapy into what was then called vegetotherapy, based on the functions of the vegetative nervous system, and which eventually was called orgone therapy. It is a functional, sex-economic approach to psychotherapy, combining psyche and soma into one unified concept. It did away with the psychoanalytic taboo of never touching a patient, substituting a physical attack by the therapist on the muscular attitudes (armoring) in the patient; thus the therapist treats the patient not only from the characterological point of view, but also physically by provoking in him a sharp contraction of the musculature in order to make the patient aware of those contractions which have become chronic. The relaxation of the bound-up energy in the musculature in whatever part of the body would often be accompanied by recall of the trauma which had led to the contraction or neurotic symptom in the first place. In this way neurotic symptoms could be attacked at the same time in their psychic and their somatic manifestations. The establishment of the healthy, normal function of the orgasm was and remained always the core of Reich's therapeutic attempts, no matter what the therapy was called. Since I am not a therapist, I refer interested readers to the article "Vegetotherapy" by Dr. Odd Havrevold, published under the pseudonym Walter Frank in the *International Journal of Sex-Economy,* Vol. I, 1942.

One thing has to be stressed, that vegetotherapy or orgone therapy has nothing to do with mechanical massage or with "masturbation therapy."

Some of the results of this new therapeutic approach were published in the *Zeitschrift* under the title "Der Orgasmusreflex" (The Orgasm Reflex) early in 1937. Later that year the article was expanded and published in book form as *Orgasmusreflex, Muskelhaltung und Koerperausdruck* (Orgasm Reflex, Posture of Musculature and Body Expression).

The development of this therapy went hand in hand with the experimental work in the laboratory. For Reich, the unity of his work in all its aspects—in the therapeutic session, in the laboratory, in social psychiatry or psychology—was always obvious, even though it did not seem that coherent to others looking at it from the outside, as it were. With good, powerful microscopes, and instruments specially constructed to permit this work, Reich investigated bioelectric tension and charge in protozoa. The same formula that regulated the orgasm in humans, the biological pulsation (tension—charge, discharge—relaxation) could be found in developing protozoa. The biological pulsation was called by Reich the core of his experimental work. He pursued it in the laboratory in his experiments with the bions and in the cancer experiments, and later outside the laboratory in the atmosphere and in outer space.

Reich's social life was intimately connected with his professional life, but it was active and there was no feeling of isolation. Camping trips, skiing trips, social gatherings in the homes of friends were fairly frequent. For the Easter holidays in 1936, Reich and his wife were invited to go with their Norwegian friends August and Lizzi Lange to their cabin in the Norwegian mountains. Both the Langes were in close touch with Reich's work, especially his social psychology, since August Lange was a sociologist. Lizzi, the artist, had made the drawing "Adolescents in Trouble" which now hangs in the entrance hall of the Orgone Energy Observatory in Maine, and is reproduced in *People in Trouble*. I would like to quote from August Lange's reminiscence of this Easter trip, as he wrote about it recently. It gives a glimpse of the unofficial, relaxed Reich, as he could be with good friends.

> When we were in the chalet in the mountains, Willy loved to hear Ravel's "Bolero." Once, after the record had been played, he told us about a dream he had for the future: He saw himself riding into Berlin as a triumphant knight mounted on a white horse, while the band played Ravel's "Bolero."—I was astonished that a man like Willy could have such a naive daydream, and at the same time I admired that he was not afraid of telling us about it!

Reich often spoke of the wonderful celebration that took place on the occasion of his fortieth birthday in March 1937, a celebration Norwegian style, with much eating and drinking, lasting for more than a day.

The work, both in its therapeutic development and in the laboratory, attracted visitors from abroad. In 1937 Dr. Roger Du Teil of the Centre Universitaire Mediterranéen in Nice came to work in the laboratory, and participated in the bion experiments which he eventually submitted to the Académie des Sciences in Paris in 1938. Du Teil came in a half-official capacity, and I remember Reich telling proudly about a dinner given at the French Embassy in Oslo in honor of Du Teil to which he and his wife were invited. The contact with Du Teil was interrupted by the outbreak of the war. Efforts by friends to find him after the war were fruitless, and one source seemed to think that he died in 1940 in the resistance movement.

The bion experiments—which after a preliminary account in the *Zeitschrift* in 1937 were explained in detail by Reich in 1938 in the book *Die Bione* (The Bions)—were based on microscopic observation of vesicular disintegration of matter under specific circumstances, and on the pulsation in the bioelectrically charged, newly developed vesicles. The development of amebae and other protozoa was filmed with a slow-motion camera attached to the microscope. There are many reels, thousands of feet, of these films in the Reich Archives. Later, in our laboratory in Forest Hills, we continued making these films, and they were not only exciting and exacting to make but just as exciting to watch.

Again, Reich was years ahead with his films of living protozoa. In 1960 the National Science Foundation gave a grant to Dr. Roman Vishniak to make a film of living protozoa. My efforts to have the Wilhelm Reich Infant Trust Fund archives put Reich's films at the disposal of Dr. Vishniak were rebuffed by the trustee; and Reich's priority, and really outstanding contribution to biology, are locked away uselessly even now.

Theoretical reflections on the reorganization of disintegrating matter led Reich to an exploration of the cancer problem, and experimental work with mice was started in Oslo in 1937. Reich's approach to any problem was never mechanical, but always functional. One step logically led to the next. Thus the potential connection between emotional block, energy stasis, tissue disintegration, and cancer development was not difficult for him to find. To the reproach that as a psychiatrist he should stay away from the somatic problems, his answer was that the energy concept cannot conceive of a split, but has to consider man as a unified biological function of psyche and soma.

The publications on sex-economy, especially the *Massenpsychologie des Faschismus,* attracted A. S. Neill of the Summerhill School in England. For years, Neill had run his school on sound, progressive principles. Neill had psychoanalytic training, but felt unsatisfied with the results. He went to Reich for vegetotherapeutic training, and joined the Institute in 1937. Neill once said that psychoanalysis had touched his head but not his heart, and that after six weeks of vegetotherapy he had experienced more emotions than in years of analysis. He has described at length his first meeting with Reich, and his experiences with vegetotherapy, in the memorial volume *Wilhelm Reich* (A. S. Neill et al. Editor Paul Ritter, The Ritter Press, 1958, Nottingham, England). He was until the end one of the closest personal friends Reich had—and I am proud to say that this friendship was extended to me and has continued all through the years.

The voluminous correspondence between them from 1938 through 1956 is fascinating and gives a wonderful picture of these two men, of the world situation as seen by them, and of the various stages of Reich's work. I shall refer to it again and again in the pages to follow.

It is noteworthy that Neill is the only one among Reich's close associates with whom Reich did not break, and with whom friendship continued in spite of the fact that Neill never made any pretense that he understood the orgone theory. Neill always said that he could follow Reich through the orgasm theory, through sex-economy, but when Reich went beyond man and his functions, Neill was no longer able to follow. And Reich accepted this because he loved and respected Neill and Neill's life work.

One of the recurrent themes in their correspondence was Reich's assertion that Neill was always searching for authorities to acknowledge Reich's discoveries, and Neill's rebuttal that he thought Reich wanted him to inform others of his work, else why did he usually send him several copies of each publication? The question of recognition seemed to have bothered both of them. My feeling is that Reich was rather ambivalent about it. He knew, and said so again and again, that he could not expect recognition in his time, especially not from those whose cherished security he was upsetting. His example was always: Could Edison, the inventor of the electric light bulb, expect recognition from the manufacturer of gas lamps? On the other hand, there was enough of the "little man" in him who wanted to be recognized and accepted by the world. He would often hang onto the smallest signs of official recognition, and stress them disproportionately, a very human and understandable reaction. I guess that Reich's hammering away at what he thought was Neill's desire for his recognition by the world was really Reich's way of reassuring himself. Dr. Ola Raknes once said that Reich may have needed to assert himself continuously because often he may have been unsure of his own theories.

During all his holidays and vacations between 1937 and 1939, Neill came to Oslo to work with Reich, and their personal friendship grew in these years. Neill tells a story that I have heard from others too, about a remark of Reich's at a social gathering during one of Neill's visits in Scandinavia. It throws some light on Reich's view of Christ primarily as martyr, and is interesting in view of the thesis which Reich was to develop many years later in his *Murder of Christ* (1953). Some friend at that party mentioned her interest in Krishnamurti and remarked that he was the most Christ-like person she had encountered. Reich's immediate question was, "If he is Christ-like, why hasn't he been murdered?"

The only other Institute member of that time who never lost touch with any of Reich's work, the only one who later came to the United States after the war to study the new developments, and who stayed with Reich to the end, is Ola Raknes. He had known of Reich and his work as early as 1928 when he, Raknes, studied psychoanalysis in Berlin; he had been among the group of Norwegian psychoanalysts who stood by Reich in Lucerne; he had been impressed by Reich as a teacher in the psychotherapeutic seminar in Oslo; and he came to Reich for training in vegetotherapy in 1936. Like Neill, he was older than Reich; also like Neill, he was willing to accept this younger man as a teacher. Ola Raknes was like a rock on which Reich could build his trust. Among the personal friends whom I have gained in the years with Reich, Ola Raknes always stands out as the calm, unperturbed and unperturbable arbiter of conflicts between Reich and other co-workers.

His coming for a visit or for work in the States could be compared with pouring oil on stormy waves. I always looked forward to his coming, and I treasure his continuing friendship. Raknes did not belong to that rather informal social group around Reich in Oslo in those years between 1936 and 1939, but rather the deep professional relationship between Reich and him developed into personal friendship during the forties and fifties.

One of the most dynamic persons in the Scandinavian group, and one of the co-founders of the Institute, was Dr. Nic (Hoel) Waal. A practicing psychoanalyst who had trained with Fenichel and Reich in Berlin and in Denmark, she was one of those who stood by Reich in Lucerne. She specialized in child psychiatry, and to the last followed Reich in his sex-economic approach. She was courageous in her defense of this work—sometimes at the cost of her professional advancement in the academic world, although she eventually succeeded in establishing a center in Oslo for the treatment of mentally disturbed children that today carries on her work as The Nic Waal Institute. She could understand the logic of the development in Reich's thinking because she had grasped the energy concept, but she thought that often his conclusions were rash and prematurely published. She thought that Reich should take the gap between his thinking and that of others more into consideration, while Reich took the attitude that once he had discovered something new, a new approach, a new theoretical concept, it was up to others to develop it in greater detail. Nic Waal was one of those who refused to follow Reich into fields for which she felt she had not been adequately prepared. She was a psychiatrist, well trained in her field; she fully accepted the sex-economic approach to psychiatry and psychotherapy; and she intended to work with it and elaborate it—which she did with great success. But her refusal to follow Reich into orgonomy brought about a break in their professional relationship and, as this was Reich's way, in their friendship. Nic later visited Reich twice, briefly, in the United States, where she had been invited to talk at the Menninger Clinic in Topeka, Kansas, and at the National Health Institute at Bethesda, Maryland about her work with children. Once, in 1956, I had a long conversation with her, and I am sure that she always thought of Reich as a friend, acknowledged him as an influential, dynamic teacher, and regretted the break in their relationship. She wrote extensively about Reich and her relationship to him in the memorial volume *Wilhelm Reich*.

I think the Scandinavian psychiatrists and psychotherapists were, as a whole, eager and willing to work with Reich in his development of new approaches to psychotherapy. But I think they felt violated, compelled by Reich to participate against their wishes in his biological experimental work. I received that feeling very distinctly in my talk with Dr. Odd Havrevold, another member of the institute in Oslo, and I think that the same is basically true for Dr. Tage Philipson, the Danish psychoanalyst who came regularly to Oslo for training and for work in the laboratory.

In 1938 Dr. Theodore P. Wolfe came from the United States to study with Reich. Wolfe was at that time an Associate in Psychiatry at Columbia University, and a psychiatrist and research physician at Presbyterian Hospital in New York. His main interest was in psychosomatic medicine. The unifying, bioenergetic concept of Reich's sex-economic theory attracted him enough to make him come to Norway to study this approach firsthand. Wolfe was of Swiss origin, spoke German fluently, and became later the translator of many of Reich's books and the director of the American Orgone Institute Press, until 1952 when a severe illness necessitated his withdrawal.

Wolfe witnessed the difficulties Reich encountered at that time in Norway. He recognized, during his travels through Europe, the signs of an impending world catastrophe and he thought that Reich's work would find better acceptance in the United States and that Reich would be much safer out of Europe. Through his contacts here he, more than anybody else, made it possible for Reich to come to the States. Together with others, he obtained a teaching contract for Reich from the New School for Social Research that, in turn, enabled Reich to receive a nonquota professor visa to emigrate to the United States in 1939.

I received much help and information in my talks with many of the former colleagues and co-workers of Reich in Scandinavia. Leunbach, Philipson, Sigurd Hoel, and Nic Waal had died before my first visit in 1963, and Arnulf Oeverland was too sick to see me at my last visit in 1966. But I did get a feeling for the period, and of what went wrong in the end: why the organization Reich had built up with so much effort disintegrated, and why his personal contact with most of his friends was broken. It is a sad and tragic story, one that was repeated again and again in Reich's life.

It began with the Norwegian newspaper campaign against Reich that broke out, according to Dr. Raknes, after a discussion of Reich's sex-economic theories in the Psychiatric Association in Oslo. Reich was accused of having misused Malinowski's findings for his own purposes—an accusation that was repudiated by Malinowski himself in a letter to the association. Raknes feels, and probably rightly so, that the Norwegian authorities, including some of the psychiatrists, were afraid that the sex-economic concepts would undermine the morals of Norwegian youth.

The campaign against Reich and his theories was intensified by the publication in 1937 of his first report on the bion experiments. The campaign consisted of a most underhanded, vicious attack by psychiatrists and biologists, as well as by fascists and communists; it was waged not in scientific journals and by scientific arguments, but in daily newspapers by innuendos, lies, and half-truths.

It is still hard to understand why this newspaper campaign was carried on so heatedly and for so long. Reich's works, mostly of a scientific nature, were published in German; they were available only to a rather selective group of people in Norway. Reich did not participate in any political activities in Norway that in themselves could have invited a reaction. His work was not publicized by himself or his co-workers in any way. The work proceeded quietly, as far as the outside world was concerned, although Reich's friend Arnulf Oeverland remarked at that time that it was "the loudest quiet" he had ever heard.

It is true, there were one or two psychoanalysts who were not on Reich's side in his conflict with the International Psychoanalytic Association, and there were some psychiatrists and biologists who were no doubt frightened by Reich's emphasis on the sexual basis of mental illness and health, and by his bioenergetic experiments, but that still does not explain this irrational outbreak of violent attacks in daily newspapers.

The fact that Oslo is not a world capital but a rather small, gossipy town increased the impact that such a smear campaign had to have on all concerned. If one's name is attacked daily in all the papers in town, one cannot help but feel persecuted, almost haunted. One does not feel like walking in the streets, pursuing daily life unconcernedly, when one imagines that everybody is looking and thinking, "there goes *that* person!" One is bound to be affected, no matter how rational he would like to feel about it. And it did affect to some degree everybody around Reich, and most of all Reich himself.

To the despair of most of his friends, Reich refused to be drawn into public argument. The campaign lasted from September 1937 through November 1938, comprising more than a hundred articles in Norway's leading newspapers, and running the gamut from "the quackery of psychoanalysis" and "the Jewish pornographer," to "God Reich creates life." Reich entered into the campaign twice. Once, at the beginning, he asked to be left alone and in peace to complete his experiments so that a detailed report could later be made. The second time he suggested a public investigation of his experiments by the proper scientific authorities, an appeal that was not accepted.

His friends and colleagues tried to set matters straight, to correct the outright lies such as assertions that he was not a medical doctor, or that he had had no training in psychoanalysis. The press showed clear bias in favor of the attackers. Many articles and letters to the editors in defense of Reich were never printed. But Reich himself would not be drawn into this mess. And he did not seem able to make anyone understand why he refused to resist this outbreak of irrational hatred against himself and his work.

It is one of the tragic aspects of Reich's life, and one of the most touching, that whenever he was faced with an irrational attack against himself and his work he would put absolute faith in the power of truth to win out in the end. He did not want to go down to the level of his attackers and he did not want anybody around him to defend him against what he later called the "emotional plague."

The other side of this attitude, however, made itself felt in his reactions to those closest to him. It was as if the restraint he had put on himself not to react to the provocation of the outside world had to give somewhere, and was loosened in violent temper attacks against first of all his wife, and then against his co-workers.

Elsa Lindenberg had succeeded at that time in building a new career, independent of Reich's work. Reich's fury was now directed against her work and against the people with whom she worked outside of his own sphere. She was closest to him, but at the same time she represented the outside world that was attacking him, and so all his reaction to the outside world was unleashed against her.

Always, in times of stress, one of Reich's very human failings came to the foreground, and that was his violent jealousy. He would always emphatically deny that he was jealous, but there is no getting away from the fact that he would accuse his wife of infidelity with any man who came to his mind as a possible rival, whether colleague, friend, local shopkeeper, or casual acquaintance. It was one of those strange contradictions in Reich's make-up, and another one that must have been founded on some basic, unresolved feelings of insecurity, because there were no reasons in fact for these jealousies. However, they seemed to provide him with what he must have felt was a rational outlet for his anger against the world.

I know what Elsa must have gone through in those days, because fifteen years later I went through the same experience. No matter how much love, devotion, and understanding one might bring to the situation, there was a point when it became a question of life or death, a matter of retaining one's own integrity and individuality or submitting completely to Reich. To save her own work, her own integrity, Elsa chose in the beginning of 1939 to leave Reich and not to accompany him to the United States, painful as this decision was for both of them.

I found very little bitterness in Elsa's recollections of her life with Reich, but much sadness and a ready acknowledgment of the insights gained. The only bitterness that I could discern had to do, again, with money matters. When Reich and Elsa separated there was no financial settlement involved. Reich felt that a woman able to earn a living had no right to alimony payments, and he always compared such payments to some kind of prostitution. He was willing to contribute to the upkeep of his children, but as I have already indicated, usually somewhat under protest and with the smallest amount possible, definitely not in keeping with his living standards. Elsa was earning a fair amount at the time of the separation. But after the German invasion she lost her job, had to go underground, and eventually fled to Sweden. Absolutely pennyless, she overcame her pride and wrote to Reich for help.

He sent her twenty-five dollars. I felt terribly ashamed when she later told me about it, because I should have realized then that she might have needed help. But I knew nothing about it. Although Reich shared most of his correspondence with me, he never once let me see Elsa's letters, and I had no idea of her situation. I knew he had sent some money to Sweden during the war, a couple of hundred dollars for Leunbach and for others, but I still don't know how it was used or distributed.

Others around Reich at the time of the newspaper campaign had to feel his violent temper too. Nic Waal—who I understand was not easily shouted down—had terrible fights with Reich, and the other colleagues and assistants began to be afraid of Reich's temper outbursts. Reich became very suspicious of people and their motives. He was afraid that people might steal some of his discoveries—a fear that stayed with him until the end of his life —and he asked his colleagues to be very careful with their papers, to sign every article clearly, to initial every page, to be sure of the priority of their, or his, every finding.

Besides the newspaper campaign, which eventually died in November 1938 when it became apparent that Reich would be leaving Norway to go to the United States, there were other reasons for the reaction against Reich within his own Scandinavian group.

Many of those who had undergone therapeutic training and treatment with him seemed to feel that he had not solved the transference situation satisfactorily. Some accused him of not being able to loosen the positive transference and let people go their own ways. Dr. Philipson called him a dictator who could not bear to let others do independent work—an accusation Reich refuted by pointing to the many psychoanalysts he had trained who had remained in the International Psychoanalytic Association and who had not followed him into his new fields. Sigurd Hoel, however, felt Reich's leaving Norway as a personal abandonment. It seems to have taken years before he felt his attachment to Reich was broken, and then as if to prove the break to himself he did not visit Reich when he came to the United States once after the war, a fact that hurt Reich very much because he still and always regarded Sigurd Hoel as a friend. And, as some friends later asked Hoel, was he really that free of his attachment if he could not face a personal encounter?

Still others felt it was the negative transference Reich had elaborated as an important aspect of his characterological therapy that led to difficulties. He provoked it in his patients, but when it came to the surface he could not stand another form of attack against himself in addition to the constant public attacks of the time. He reacted, as one of them put it, by "slapping me down to such an extent that it took years to recover from it."

When Reich finally left Norway in August 1939 the reaction of almost all his co-workers, for whatever reason, was one of being freed from a loyalty to a man and a work that had become an oppression.

When the war broke out, Reich's remaining personal contact with the Scandinavian group was interrupted. Reich was so engrossed in the early forties with the new developments of orgone research and the building up of the institute in the United States that he had little or no understanding of the social, political, and economic situation of his friends in Scandinavia. Many had been in concentration camps, in prison, in the underground movement. Quite a few had to flee to Sweden. Most lost everything and had to rebuild their lives after the holocaust. Under these circumstances they could not muster much interest and enthusiasm in the orgone theory and the orgone accumulators, even when contact was again possible after the war. Reich could not understand this, and felt let down by them.

Some of them had helped Reich financially with the cost of transferring the laboratory to the United States. When they now asked for repayment of what they had regarded as loans, they were informed that this money represented their contribution to the research fund. Reich still thought of them as the well-to-do psychotherapists he had left, without having an inkling of what they had gone through, or what their economic situation was like at the end of the war.

All of these were reasons for the breaking up of the institute in Scandinavia. Left were Ola Raknes as the representative of the new development, and Nic Waal with her institute for psychiatric treatment of children working on sex-economic principles. The others worked on as private psychotherapists, most of them developing their own adaptations of vegetotherapy, withdrawing completely from any further direct contact with Reich and his work.

Talking to them now, they all seem to understand the tragedy of Reich's life. There is very little animosity left, but rather a general acknowledgment of the many positive things they learned from Reich about handling their own lives and those of their children and patients. The impact of Reich's work and personality has without doubt left its mark on all of them.

One almost gets the feeling that each time Reich had to start anew he went up to greater heights, to more important discoveries; but it becomes apparent that in the end the disappointments became correspondingly deeper, and harder to take. In Norway he felt he had come closer to the basis of the biological energy than ever before, both in human beings through the development of the new therapeutic approach, and in simple protoplasm through his biological experiments with the bions. But the public campaign against him had cost him more than friends : it had destroyed the first organization that had rested entirely upon his own work. Certainly, the attack had come from without—but the question remained why the organization was not strong enough to withstand such an attack. Always, previously, Reich had been the outsider working in an organization not his own. This was different, and I think Reich felt the difference.

In the spring of 1939, Reich received a contract from the New School for Social Research in New York appointing him associate professor of medical psychology. On the basis of this he expected to leave Oslo immediately, but the visa was delayed. In the meantime, the laboratory in Oslo was dismantled and packed for shipment to New York. Since some of the experimental cultures had to be kept going, one of Reich's laboratory assistants, Gertrud Gaasland, accompanied the laboratory equipment to New York in May. With Dr. Wolfe's help she prepared for the re-establishment of the laboratory there.

While Reich was waiting rather lonesomely in Oslo for his visa, he was filled with expectations for the continuation of his work in the States. He wrote in one of his letters to Gertrud Gaasland that he felt the transfer to the States to be a logical step in the development of his work; that the old world had become static and that he felt the atmosphere in the States to be more alive. He compared it to the Berlin atmosphere in 1930, much more receptive to his ideas and theories. He explained his optimism with his feeling that in the general shift of social emphasis from the importance of the machine to the importance of the human being "our work is going to be indispensable." He concluded one letter by saying that in spite of the terrible tribulations to which mankind was again and again exposed, he, Reich, had "infinite trust in reason, just because I am so familiar with what can disturb it."

Every one of his letters during this waiting period, from the beginning of June to the middle of August 1939, shows his indestructible optimism, his preoccupation with social and scientific theories, his great worries about the continuation of the laboratory experiments, and his concern over financial problems involved in setting up a new laboratory in the United States.

In these letters he also tries to clarify his relationship to his friends and co-workers in Scandinavia, and to understand why things did go wrong. He mentions on more than one occasion the many *Dummheiten* (foolish errors) he had made in handling people, and in handling his reactions to them, and he seems to have understood that his demands on others were generally unreasonable.

The Reich household in Oslo had likewise broken up. Elsa had left to stay with friends; the good old cook who had been very much attached to Reich—she sent us a lovely children's book after the war when she learned of Peter's birth—had to find another place. The library and some of the Norwegian furniture and furnishings were shipped to New York. Reich's beloved automobile was sold to a friend in Norway. Reich lived the last six weeks alone in the house of some friends. Most everybody had gone away on vacation. He often told how he lived mostly on baked beans out of a can and frankfurters. He was the worst cook possible, and I imagine it was hard for him to fend for himself. On the other hand, he did not care to go out to restaurants where people knew him and stared at him.

He left Oslo on August 19, 1939, on the *Stavanger Fjord,* and arrived in New York just a few days before the outbreak of the war in Europe.

U.S.A.: 1939–1950
(First Decade)

Shortly after his arrival in New York, Reich moved his laboratory and equipment to a rented house in Forest Hills, Long Island. The children had come to the United States with their mother Annie in 1938 and were living in New York. With the help of Dr. Wolfe and Reich's assistant Gertrud Gaasland, the house soon hummed with activity, although it was actually not very ideal for use as a "workshop." It had a small basement which was used for animal experiments, and a large room on the first floor which served mainly as Reich's office but also had to function as dining room, living room, and as accommodation for the seminar every other week. The regular dining room adjoining the kitchen was made into a laboratory with microscopes, oscillograph, electroscopes, and other instruments. The maid's room on the other side of the kitchen was used both as office and as preparation room for the laboratory cultures and media. The two bedrooms on the top floor were shared by Gertrud and the maid, and of the three small rooms on the second floor one was used as Reich's bedroom and the others for psychotherapy sessions.

I met Reich in the beginning of October 1939 through Gertrud. She had been a political refugee in Norway, and between 1933 and 1938 had several times visited Paris where I had made her acquaintance. Upon her coming to New York in May, we renewed our acquaintance and met frequently at the home of mutual friends. She always spoke with enthusiasm about her work with Reich. Although I did not understand the first thing about it, she insisted that I come over to see the laboratory and meet Reich. I lived within walking distance of Forest Hills, and I remember walking over one Saturday afternoon. I met Reich briefly and was very much impressed by him, even a bit awed. He was a striking figure with his grey hair, ruddy complexion, and white coat. He showed me the laboratory, the house, and invited me to have a glass of wine.

I was surprised when a few days later Reich called and asked me to come over because Gertrud was not feeling well. I went over and found that Gertrud really did not need me, but that Reich had wanted to talk with me. He came to town fairly frequently after these first meetings; we met after my office work, had dinner— mostly in Italian restaurants which he preferred—went to a movie and occasionally to a concert. He introduced me to some of his colleagues whom he saw socially—such as the psychoanalyst Dr. Walter Briehl and his family—and I remember a Sunday drive with the Briehls to Jones Beach which impressed Reich and me, for we both knew little of New York's surroundings at that time.

Reich talked to me of his children and of Elsa. He explained his separation from her, saying that she had wanted to be independent and had feared that she might not be able to build up her own work again in the States, especially since she did not speak English very well. He told me that he was still very much attached to her, but that the relationship had come to an end.

I was working in an office at that time, rather unhappily, hoping to start studies soon for a more satisfactory occupation, possibly in social work. Reich knew that I was unhappy in my work, that I wanted to do something more meaningful. In December he asked whether I would be interested in working for him. His work was growing and Gertrud could not handle it all alone. I could take over the secretarial work and the bookkeeping end, and Gertrud could slowly introduce me to the work in the laboratory. It sounded very exciting and interesting. I understood that it would mean, at the same time, a closer personal relationship.

It did. I became Reich's wife on Christmas Day, 1939, and began work for him on January 2, 1940. The household consisted of Reich and myself, Gertrud, and a maid. I took over the household and the secretarial work, and helped Gertrud in the laboratory with the mice and the bion cultures. I learned how to make culture media, how to sterilize the glassware, and—most enjoyable—how to use a microscope. To get a more thorough grounding for the research work, I took a course in laboratory technique and bacteriology in 1940–1941 at one of the special schools for laboratory assistants in New York.

Both Gertrud and I assisted Reich by showing slides and films when he began his lectures at the New School for Social Research in the spring of 1940. I needed to attend Reich's lectures on "Biological Aspects of Character Formation" as background for my work, and to help me better understand Reich's basic concepts.

Reich was always punctual for his lectures. We would usually be in town at least half an hour before the beginning of class, and often we would meet Malinowski—who was also lecturing at the New School—for coffee or sometimes dinner before the evening lecture. Reich could not tolerate unpunctuality. If someone came late to his lecture he would interrupt what he was saying, glare silently and ferociously at the latecomer until he or she was seated, and only then continue. No one came late twice. Except Eva. It was one of the few faults he found with his older daughter—that she was always late, no matter where. When we went to a concert or a play with her, we would leave her ticket at the door because Reich could not bear waiting and being late himself.

A few of the people attending the first lecture courses at the New School later became members of the seminar. Among the eight to ten people in this seminar on the "Psychological Approach to

Psychosomatic Research" were some psychotherapists, research physicians, and educators. The relationship of Reich to the members of the seminar was friendly but formal. Some of them had been in his Vienna Psychoanalytic Seminar. As I have mentioned before, he maintained some social life with them, with an occasional dinner party, or a drink after the lectures at the New School.

One of Reich's trainees, a young research physician from Presbyterian Hospital in New York, helped by providing connections to breeders of research animals. I learned a great deal from him about handling animals. He introduced me to the director of the research-animal department at Presbyterian Hospital, who took me on a tour of her facilities and gave me much valuable information.

Reich's relationship with his two children, Eva and Lore, was strained. There was some fear and antagonism in both of them. I often had the feeling that they felt they were doing something improper by being with us, and it made everybody uncomfortable. Their insecurity probably came from the strained relationship between their parents, and from the many unpleasant rumors about Reich circulating in psychoanalytic circles. We had the most enjoyable times with them when we took them, sometimes with their friends, on Sunday drives to Jones Beach which had become our regular haunt, or through Westchester to the Poundridge Reservation.

Among the people Reich saw socially in the early forties were some old Viennese friends. But they were not in any way connected with his work, and he became easily impatient with just social talk. He also tried to avoid renewed contact through them with the Viennese psychoanalysts most of whom he felt were antagonistic.

We went fairly frequently to Philharmonic concerts in those early years and even went dancing once or twice, but Reich would not join me when I went to chamber music performances because he knew that many of his old Viennese circle might be there. We went very often to the movies where in the anonymity of the darkened theater Reich could completely relax, regardless of what kind of film it was. His taste in films was rather naïve and not very discriminating. Westerns, musicals, comedies, tragedies—he went to see them all. He had some favorites among the film actors of the forties: Alice Faye, Greer Garson, Spencer Tracy, James Stewart. But with all his naïveté and enjoyment, he was always interested in the impact of the movies on the mores of society. He pointed out again and again how any kind of natural sexual enjoyment, even if protrayed as most desirable, was inevitably punished in the end if it did not comply with the strict and generally accepted code of behavior.

Reich was conservative when it came to going places. Once he liked a place he went back again and again. We usually went to the same Italian restaurant in the city, the same restaurant in Forest Hills, and we went regularly to Jones Beach or the Poundridge Reservation.

Reich had made it clear when we got married that he was marrying me, not my family. He met some of my cousins in New York once or twice and he had some correspondence with my brother who was familiar with his work and very interested in it, but he was definitely not a son-in-law to my parents. This was a shock to them and they worried a great deal about me, although I was thirty years old by that time and this was my second marriage. The difficulty was lessened by the fact that they lived in England, and the problem of family relations did not matter greatly. Reich was aware though that I was attached to my parents, and I shall always remember the warm, loving, and supportive way in which he told me of my father's death in April 1940. The telegram had come in the middle of the afternoon while there were patients around. Reich read it and put it away without saying anything, and I wondered what it could possibly be. After everyone had left, he sat down with me, told me the news, put his arms around me and told me to let myself go and cry; he was there right with me and understood my sorrow.

Reich met some of my old friends from Germany and France, but he was jealous of them to a certain extent. Although most of them knew Reich's *Mass Psychology,* and of his mental hygiene work in Germany, they did not know or understand the work he was so vitally interested in at the moment and he could not take time away from it for purely social reasons. After a while I lost the close touch I had had with my family here and with my friends, and I saw them only once or twice a year. First, because my time was so filled with work that it was hard to get away, and second, because I felt that Reich did not want me to keep these old ties.

In July 1940 Reich decided to take a month's vacation. We started on a camping trip through New England, with his Norwegian tent, sleeping bags, and other equipment. The first week in Vermont and New Hampshire was beautiful and we camped by little streams in the woods, but then it started to rain and we discovered that the tent leaked badly. We drove from the White Mountains to Maine and arrived at Mooselookmeguntic Lake where we found, on a private estate, a small log cabin—a guide's camp—for rent. The big house was empty and we were all alone to enjoy the peace and quiet of the lake, with not much more comfort than the tent but with at least a dry floor and roof.

Reich made some important observation in the dry atmosphere of the region at that time, and decided it was the ideal spot for combining work and vacation. For the past few years he had been searching for an effective means to make the biological energy, the orgone energy, visible and usable for physical and therapeutic experimentation. During this short vacation he thought he had found those means through electroscopic measurements and observations made with binoculars. We contemplated coming back the next year, and found near the guide's camp a small log cabin that was for sale. We talked to the owner, who was willing to sell the cabin but said that the old Maine guide who had built it would have to approve of the new owners. So we went to see old man Templeton, the guide, and talked with him. Before long he and Reich were in the midst of a deep philosophical discussion about man and nature; there was no doubt that Templeton approved of us as the new owners.

That was the beginning of our taking roots in the town of Rangeley, Maine. The cabin, which Reich named Orgonotoc Lodge, became our Maine headquarters until 1946 when we moved to Orgonon on Dodge Pond, still in the same town.

As I write these lines I am sitting just a few steps away from our first living place on Mooselookmeguntic. There is something very peaceful and quiet in the permanency of the sights, the smells, and the sounds of this spot. The silhouette of the tall pines against the sky and the lake, the expanse of the lake itself, and the outline of the mountains in the distance; the piney woods smell and the scent of the new-mown hay, the song of the birds, the chattering of the squirrels and chipmunks, the lapping of the waves—all remain the same, year after year, no matter how the world and people change, no matter what turmoil and unrest there is elsewhere. I think that this permanency, this peacefulness of nature, is what made Reich come back here again and again, is what gave him some of the strength to withstand the adversities of so many years. Whether at Mooselookmeguntic or at Orgonon with its colorful meadows, there was and is a special peaceful and reassuring continuity in the familiar landscape.

Back in New York, Reich's psychotherapeutic work with his trainees continued and the experimental work with the energy phenomena received new impetus through the observations made in Maine. His work with electroscopic measurements was intensified and in the fall of 1940 led him to the construction of the first orgone energy accumulators, to be used experimentally on mice. Reich had observed that organic material attracts orgone energy and absorbs it, while metal attracts but repels it. He had the first mouse accumulator built on that principle: a small box, not larger than a cigar box, with Cellotex on the outside and sheet iron on the inside, with airholes in the lid. Later on he had larger accumulators for humans built on the same principle, with alternating layers of various organic and metallic substances, and with an open window in the door to permit circulation of air.

The first small mouse accumulators were used in experiments on cancerous mice. Until then the experiments had been done with direct injections of bion solutions or with serum obtained from rabbits. The experiments on mice and on human beings with the orgone energy accumulator were described by Reich in detail in an article "Experimental Orgone Therapy of the Cancer Biopathy," published in the *International Journal of Sex-Economy and Orgone Research* Vol. II, 1943, and later included in Reich's book *The Discovery of the Orgone,* Vol. II, *The Cancer Biopathy,* Orgone Institute Press, 1948.

The first accumulator to be used on humans was constructed in December 1940. It was put in the basement and I remember the excitement when we all took turns sitting in it and upon having our temperatures taken saw Reich's prediction of a rise in temperature come true.

The work in the laboratory was very demanding and Reich was

a hard taskmaster. The records on each mouse had to be kept meticulously as to every detail of treatment; the electroscopic measurements had to be timed with a stop watch to fractions of seconds. At times I had the feeling that our whole life was ruled by the stop watch.

With the development of the accumulator Reich got deeper and deeper into the realm of biophysics. I think that he felt desperately alone. There were good psychotherapists around him, but no one who understood where he was going or the significance of his discoveries. He needed to talk and I was there to listen, but I did not understand the implications of what he talked about and neither did anyone else around him.

Despite the bad experiences he had had when he took his discoveries to authorities in any specific field, he decided that he had to discuss the energy phenomena he had found with a physicist. At the end of December 1940 he wrote a letter to Einstein asking for an appointment to discuss these findings with him.

I am not able to discuss the scientific conclusions or any of the other details of what Reich would later call the Einstein Affair. I do not understand and therefore cannot judge the scientific principles involved. Despite all the arguments and materials that Reich and his assistants assembled to prove that Einstein's sudden indifference was part of a general communist-inspired conspiracy against Reich's work, I do not believe that such a conspiracy existed. I know that several of the individuals involved in attacking and tearing down Reich's work were communists. Lots of people in intellectual circles at that time were communists. But this, to my mind, does not add up to a conspiracy. My personal opinion of the matter is that Einstein saw the phenomena, may have had an inkling of their significance, but was unwilling to get involved in a highly controversial scientific discovery at a time when he was deeply engrossed with developing atomic energy. I am going to confine myself here to only those human reactions that I very clearly remember and that have to do with Reich the man rather than with Reich, the scientist.

Reich was very excited, and had his approach to Einstein carefully prepared when he left for Princeton on January 13, 1941, around noontime. He returned very late that night, close to midnight. I had waited up for him, and he was so full of excitement and impressions that we talked far into the early morning hours. He told me that the conversation with Einstein had been extremely friendly and cordial, that Einstein was easy to talk to, that their conversation had lasted almost five hours. Einstein was willing to investigate the phenomena that Reich had described to him, and a special little accumulator would have to be built and taken to him. Reich told me that Einstein evidently had enjoyed looking through the small instrument Reich had taken along—an orgonoscope in which one could observe the manifestations of orgone energy—and that he had left it with him. When Reich told him about the most important finding, the temperature difference inside and outside the accumulator, the reason for Reich's visit to him—Einstein said that if it were true it would be a "bomb." Reich was pleased that after the long talk Einstein had taken him for a physicist and when told that he was a psychiatrist had asked, "What else do you do?"

Reich spoke of how exciting it was to talk to someone who knew the background of these physical phenomena, who had an immediate grasp of the implications. He started to daydream of possibilities for working with Einstein at the Institute of Advanced Studies, where he would be in a community of scientists on a level where he, Reich, would not always be the giving one, with everybody else taking, as it was in his own institute, but where he would find a give and take on his own level. He had wanted for a long time to be done with the world of the neurotic, to devote himself solely to the biophysical aspects of his discovery. But unless he could work within a framework that would support his research he was obliged for financial reasons to continue with the psychotherapeutic training in character-analytic therapy. He spoke that night of such possibilities, and hung onto this daydream for the next few weeks.

During the next days Reich was busy preparing the experimental setup for Einstein, speculating on Einstein's reactions to the observations with the little instrument he had left with him. On February 1, Reich took the experimental apparatus to Princeton. He was again very much impressed by Einstein and his interest in this work.

What followed then is a matter for scientists to evaluate. Einstein wrote that he had confirmed Reich's findings, but gave a different interpretation of the temperature difference. In a very lengthy, well-documented scientific paper based on a series of carefully executed experiments, Reich refuted without rancor Einstein's interpretation. Einstein, for reasons unknown, never responded. On the other hand, Einstein had expressly stated that he did not wish to have the matter aired in the open. Much later, in 1953, the correspondence was published by Reich in a limited edition titled *The Einstein Affair,* as part of Reich's biographical material.

Reich's personal reaction to Einstein's sudden silence was one of bafflement, which gradually turned to deep disappointment. Reich's dream of becoming a member of a community of scientists, which he had spoken of again and again during those weeks in January and February, was not going to come true.

But Reich emerged quickly from his disappointment and from what I believe he felt intensely as a personal rejection by Einstein; with his usual resiliency, he began to concentrate on establishing his own work under the name of Bion and Cancer Research Laboratory (later, Orgone and Cancer Research Laboratories and finally incorporated as Orgone Institute Research Laboratories, Inc.). He prepared with Dr. Wolfe's help for the development of a publishing house of his own in the United States to handle all the material that was rapidly accumulating, a continuation of the European Sexpol-Verlag.

In Norway, Reich had started to work on the concept of work democracy as opposed to all political party organizations and ideologies. He continued to elaborate on his theory and wrote several articles which were later incorporated in the English edition of *Mass Psychology.* They first appeared in the *International Journal of Sex-Economy and Orgone Research* in 1943. In his letters to Neill in 1941 he explained some of these ideas. Work democracy, he maintained, is the natural organization of human interrelations; such interrelations, he said, cannot be organized like a political party. Bureaucracy in any form would not be necessary in a work democracy because the working process on any level would administrate its life quite on its own. Reich thought the only hope for the world after the war lay in real work democracy, based on science, work, and natural love. He thought that efforts toward true democracy were greater in the United

States than those under socialism in Europe. He predicted early in 1941 that the postwar world would have to be built on work-democratic principles unless it were to become again a pre-war world with the next war within ten or twenty years. He wrote about moralistic man within a culture that makes bombs and poison gas, that tolerates prisons and politicians, and he believed that this world was destroying itself.

In February or March 1941, Reich's emphasis on work democracy versus political parties and political ideologies led to a sudden break with his assistant Gertrud Gaasland, following a violent discussion about these problems. I remember that the dispute started in the car going home after a lecture at the New School, and continued late into the night. Gertrud left the next day, and eventually she went back to Norway. Because of Reich's attitude of "you are with me or against me," I could not keep in touch with her and did not see her again until my visit to Norway in 1966.

Early in 1941, Reich got in touch with a patent lawyer and tried to obtain a patent for the orgone energy accumulator. As with all patent applications, this was a long drawn-out process. The patent was never granted, but Reich hoped that with the application he might at least safeguard his priority.

In addition to his lecture course at the New School in the spring of 1941, Reich continued the work in the laboratory with experiments on mice and soon with the first human cancer patients. The experiments with humans started in May 1941. These patients, referred by physicians, were all regarded as hopeless cases in the last stages of the disease. Their families had been informed that this was only an experimental treatment and that no miracle cure could be expected. The results of these experiments were published in the article mentioned before. I was impressed by the infinite patience, the gentleness with which Reich treated these cancer patients, and by the great amount of time he spent with each individual.

At that time, we began to have trouble with our neighbors. They objected to our letting the hedge around the house grow high; they objected to our having a Negro assistant, a young biology student who studied for a while with Reich and, of course, shared our meals; they objected to the "rats" in our basement and they transmitted these complaints to our landlord. He sent an investigator who could find no reason for the complaints and was very much surprised to find our mice confined to securely closed boxes neatly arranged on shelves. He had expected to find a basement overrun by vermin. However, we felt our privacy invaded by one particular neighbor who continued to observe our every move, and we did not want to live at the mercy of a landlord's whims. Anyway, the house was rather far from any public transportation and not too well suited for our purposes. We decided to look for a more suitable building, to be bought in the fall.

In the summer months of July and August we went back to Maine, this time with a lot of work to be done during vacation. We continued to live with the electroscopes and the inevitable stop watch, and we took along some of the mice because we were in the midst of an experiment. There were innumerable manuscripts to be typed and routine correspondence to be attended to. Reich had electricity put into the cabin so he could work with the microscopes, but this was our only luxury. The icehouse had been filled by Mr. Templeton during the winter, and wood chopped for the stove and fireplace. Our refrigerator was an old-fashioned icebox, and I cooked on a small kerosene stove. We had cold water, pumped up from the lake, and enjoyed the luxury of warm water when the fireplace was going because Templeton, in his ingenuity, had put some coils of water pipe at the back of the fireplace. It was good to live and work on the lake, and we enjoyed it thoroughly. We had occasional visitors, a Viennese friend of Reich's with whom I had become good friends too, and Dr. Wolfe who came up for a week to rest and to discuss the progress of the translations and publications.

Reich loved to bathe in the lake but he was not a good swimmer, while I enjoy swimming and have always been good at it. This led to my discovery of a curious fear for the safety of others that was typical of Reich. He would stand at the shore, and whenever he thought I was swimming too far out he would order me back. Neill also remembers Reich's fear for others. Once, in 1948, when he and Reich were watching the construction of the Orgone Energy Observatory at Orgonon, Neill mounted a ladder to get a better view. Reich implored him to come down, to watch out, claiming that it was not safe. In the same way, Reich was always much more worried than I about our son when the boy started to climb rocks and trees. I shall never forget the day when Reich's daughter Eva, her husband Bill Moise, some of their friends, our son Peter who was about eight years old, and I decided to follow the Appalachian Trail up Saddleback Mountain. We left early in the morning and hoped to be back in the afternoon, but it took us longer than anticipated. We were back by nightfall, and Bill Moise went to the nearest telephone to tell Reich that we had returned safely. Reich was terribly worried and very angry, almost ready to call out the Forest Rangers. When we finally came back to the house there was such a scene that it spoiled the beauty of the day for all of us.

We returned to New York in September and began immediately to look for a house. People must have thought us rather peculiar, because we were not so much interested in dining rooms and living rooms as in the basement. It did not take long to find a suitable home. It was in easy walking distance from subway and train stations, with a bus stop on the next corner. The large basement with a separate laundry room was ideal for laboratory purposes and had a separate entrance. The rooms in the house were larger than in the old one. Reich could have his library in his study, out of the way of the laboratory and the various household activities. As before, the dining room was used for microscopy, and later on for X-ray work. The living room became a combination waiting room, office, and dining room. It was an ordinary, one-family brick corner house on Sixty-ninth Avenue in Forest Hills, one block from the Forest Hills Stadium. But it is strange what some people saw in it. One reporter called it a "considerable establishment;" another one thought it was "tucked away in an obscure corner near a gas house."

We moved into the house on October 1, 1941. Reich was looking forward to a period of undisturbed activity. The Orgone Institute and the Orgone Institute Press were to be organized, and a great deal of the experimental work had to be written up for publication. A very important article on biophysical functionalism was in preparation; it explained how the energy concept unifies the various disciplines into one functional body—to the dismay of the mechanistic, split-up specialists in those diverse fields.

But Reich was not to be left in peace.

On Sunday, December 7, we had driven out to Jones Beach in the morning. Like millions of other Americans we had heard the news of Pearl Harbor and Roosevelt's declaration of war over our car radio on the way home. During the next few days we heard of arrests of enemy aliens, but neither one of us thought that we would be in any way considered as enemies. It has never been satisfactorily explained by any government agency on what basis Reich was arrested, but on December 12, 1941, at two o'clock in the morning, two FBI agents rang the doorbell and produced orders to take Reich into custody. Reich was furious that they would not let him call his lawyer, and especially that they would not even let him go alone to the bathroom to get dressed. They didn't allow him to take even his toilet articles with him into custody, and they would not tell me where they were taking him. As soon as they had left I got in touch with our lawyer, who found out the next day that Reich was on Ellis Island. The lawyer was allowed to see him there and took along some of the things he needed.

Reich had to sleep that first night on a spread-out newspaper in a big hall on Ellis Island together with hundreds of Bund people. Since his skin condition always got worse with any excitement, he demanded to see a physician. The doctor agreed that he needed special care and had him transferred to the hospital ward where I was permitted to visit him twice a week. Dr. Wolfe and the lawyer tried their utmost to find out what the charge was against Reich. Wolfe went several times to Washington and the lawyer insisted on an immediate hearing, but despite all efforts the hearing did not take place until December 26. Eventually, after Reich had threatened the authorities with a hunger strike, he was unconditionally released on January 5, 1942.

The day after Reich's arrest two FBI men came to the house with a search warrant. They were interested only in Reich's study and the library. I insisted on being present while they looked through the manuscripts and proceeded to pull every book from the shelves and shake it out. I still don't know what they expected to find, but my respect for FBI men has been rather low ever since one of them remarked during this procedure that he could not understand how an educated man could mess up his books the way Reich did with blue and red pencil marks.

They finally found three incriminating books which they took along: Hitler's *Mein Kampf,* Trotzky's *My Life,* and a Russian alphabet for children that Reich had bought in Russia in 1929. At the hearing Reich was questioned about his possession of the Hitler and Trotzky books, and it was not so easy as one might think to convince the judge that if a psychiatrist studies mass behavior he has to know something about those people on the right and on the left who manipulate the masses.

The entire episode was sad. Reich wanted to see his children, but everybody was so afraid of getting involved in a process not at all understood that their mother would not let them go with me to Ellis Island or even visit with me in Forest Hills. My relatives, who hardly knew Reich, could not understand what was happening and did not want to have anything to do with the matter. There were a few of Reich's students and trainees who offered to help. Reich's lawyer and Dr. Wolfe made great efforts, and our young laboratory assistant of that time offered to stay with me during Reich's absence so that I would not be all alone in the big house. She was with us only a short time, but throughout those trying three weeks she and her family were among the few people on whom I could rely.

Once Reich was released he rated as a friendly alien because of his Austrian citizenship, but as I had been born in Germany, I became an enemy alien. This meant that Reich needed special permission from the government to keep and work with his cameras and film apparatus, because of the enemy alien in the house; the permission was granted. All during the war years I had to apply for special permission to travel between New York and Maine, while Reich was free to come and go as he pleased. It is not always easy to understand the workings of bureaucracy.

Reich gave his last lecture course at the New School for Social Research in the spring of 1941. Many of the students of these lecture courses came to Reich personally for further study. It was at this time that several of the physicians, among them Dr. Walter Briehl, suggested that Reich take the New York State medical licensing examination which would allow him to practice medicine, and enable him to avoid any complications with the law in this regard. But Reich absolutely refused this advice. He maintained, logically, that if he had been invited to the United States as a professor to teach medical psychology and psychotherapeutic techniques to physicians, the implication was clearly that he must know more than his students. Therefore there was no need for a special license to practice medicine. Furthermore, he had not been practicing medicine for many years and was not about to open an office in New York. He was limiting himself to training professional workers—physicians, psychologists, educators, social workers, clergymen—and to pure research. He had his M.D. degree, was well known in academic circles, and that was enough. Dr. Briehl tried to persuade Reich that the licensing exam was just a formality, and he predicted that Reich would get into difficulties if he insisted on his refusal. But Reich remained adamant. This, together with Dr. Briehl's disappointment in not finding in Reich the same person he had known in Vienna, led to his withdrawal from further work with Reich.

Unfortunately, Dr. Briehl's prediction came true. In each of the later attacks on Reich's work the question of the license was inevitably raised. I think though that Reich was correct in his refusal. He did not practice medicine in the usual sense, and all through the years worked only with professional workers who came for training, or with patients in research projects.

The next few years, the early forties, were comparatively free from outside interference and the work progressed well. There were a great number of new developments.

The experimental treatment of cancer patients continued. They came regularly to Forest Hills to use the accumulators and for bloodtests. Only at the end of 1942, when collapsible accumulators were constructed that could be shipped rather easily, were patients able to use them at home. There were only five or six of these accumulators available at first; their number increased slowly to about twelve by the end of 1943.

The experimental treatment was free, but it was always made clear to patients or their families that contributions to the Orgone Research Fund were appreciated, even if the contribution amounted to only a few dollars. Reich used to say that anything given absolutely free was always debased in the eyes of the receiver, and that a small contribution of two or three dollars a month should be within the reach of everybody. However, there were always some patients who received both accumulator and treatment completely free of charge.

The construction of the accumulator did not change very much over the years except that more layers were added to increase the strength. The theoretical explanation of its effect on biological organisms, very briefly and in lay terms, is this: The concentrated orgone energy interacts with the biological energy of the organism, strengthening it and thus enabling it to fight any disturbance in the energy flow. The use of the accumulator was never intended as a cure for all ills, but rather as a means to strengthen the body in its fight against disease. Over the years, the use of the accumulator has been so often misrepresented and misinterpreted that the original use for which it was intended has been almost obscured.

The laboratory hummed with activity. There were experiments continuing with bions and with protozoa. One full-time laboratory assistant besides myself, and several volunteers and part-time assistants, worked on the biological aspects of Reich's discoveries, while he and a young Austrian refugee who had a background in physics worked on the development of energy field phenomena and gravitational problems.

I remember a curious side of Reich's relationship to those whom he regarded as employees rather than as co-workers or students. If one of the co-workers or students became too sure of himself or too overbearing Reich would have no compunction in kicking him out, telling him in no uncertain words that his behavior was not to be tolerated. But when it came to the dismissal of an unsatisfactory employee, Reich absolutely refused to do the firing. That job was relegated to me as the administrator, and although I also abhorred dismissing anyone, I had to do it. Often when we were in agonies about the fact that somebody had to be fired, it turned out that the person was relieved to get away to either a better paying or less exacting job.

Orgone Institute Press began its activity with the publication of the first volume of *The Discovery of the Orgone: The Function of the Orgasm,* in 1942. This was not simply a translation of Reich's earlier German book of the same title, but included several articles which had later appeared in the *Zeitschrift,* such as "Psychological Contact and Vegetative Streamings," and "The Orgasm Reflex." The International Institute for Sex-Economy and Orgone Research was reconstituted in the United States as a continuation of the European institute, and the first *International Journal of Sex-Economy and Orgone Research* was published in 1942. Many of

Reich's articles that appeared in this journal between 1942 and 1943 were later included in the second volume of *The Discovery of the Orgone* in 1948, and in an enlarged and revised edition of the German *Mass Psychology of Fascism* (1946). The latter book contained Reich's later articles on his work-democratic concept, and a long revision of his appraisal of developments in the Soviet Union.

A considerable number of psychologists and psychiatrists came for training in psychiatric orgone therapy, as the development of Reich's character-analytic vegetotherapy was now called. Some of them were already established in private practice, others were working in one or the other of the state hospitals in New York and New Jersey. Teachers from private and public schools wished to be trained, especially those working with very young children or with adolescents and who felt the need for better understanding of themselves and their charges. Gymnastic teachers and dancers were intrigued with Reich's concept of muscular armoring. They were interested in developing the therapeutic aspect of gymnastics with both children and adults, and they needed training. In the beginning of this period only Reich himself and Wolfe practiced psychiatric orgone therapy, but by 1944 there were others who had been trained and Reich complained that psychiatric orgone therapy was fast becoming a good means to earn much money. It worried him a great deal. He was afraid that some of his students and trainees might sacrifice the orgasm theory for easy money and affluence.

The informality of the Scandinavian institute, where most assistants were addressed by first names, had given way to a much more formal atmosphere. Any woman working for Reich, in the laboratory or in any other capacity, had to use her maiden name. We had several assistants who got married or divorced, and Reich refused to be bothered with the resulting name changes. So we all worked under our maiden names, and although socially I was Mrs. Reich, most co-workers knew me as Miss Ollendorff. Reich called most of the female assistants Miss So-and-So, and in keeping with European custom addressed his male assistants by their last names only, without the Mister. He called all physicians who came to him for training Doctor ——, including Dr. Wolfe, although on rare occasions he would call him just Wolfe. This day-to-day formality was extended to me also, and very few of the assistants and co-workers called me by my first name. Reich never understood that the American custom of calling people by their first names after slight acquaintance did not imply an uncalled-for familiarity as it does in Europe. He was displeased and suspicious of the motives of anyone calling me Ilse after short acquaintance.

Reich had difficulty in adjusting to the American scene in other respects, too. He transferred certain European academic standards directly to America with unhappy results. In Europe, for instance, a teacher at a *Gymnasium* or a *lycée* has a rather high academic standing. He is often addressed as Professor and usually has a Ph.D. or its equivalent. He frequently teaches courses at university level. In America a high school teacher usually has a master's degree, and his status in the academic world cannot compare to that of a college professor. Reich did not know this, and he very definitely overestimated the academic importance of some of the teachers who came to him for training. He expected of them more in the way of academic background than they had, and as a result he was often disappointed when they dropped out of the work. Their ability to grasp the highly complex theories did not match the degree of their enthusiasm.

During the summer months we continued to work in Maine. Reich found the dry air of the Rangeley region especially valuable for his biophysical experiments, and spent more and more time there during the summer. Wolfe, who needed to confer extensively with Reich on the editing of the journal and translations, found a cabin on Mooselookmeguntic Lake almost adjacent to Reich's and began to spend more time there in the summer. Reich gave serious thought to acquiring a larger place where an experimental laboratory could be built, and we explored the vicinity for a suitable spot. I think it was our friend Jo Jenks, the sculptress who later made the bust of Reich, who discovered in the summer of 1942 the abandoned farm which was to become Orgonon. The farm was part woodland and part meadow, and a completely broken-down farmhouse and large barn still stood on the land. The hill which Reich thought would be the ideal site for a future observatory had a beautiful view of the mountains and lakes. There was a well and a spring on the land and about half a mile of shoreline on Dodge Pond. I don't remember how much we paid for the land, but it was inexpensive, $1,500 or $2,000 for about 280 acres.

At first Reich thought that the old barn could be converted into a laboratory, but the building was too old and had to be torn down. However, when the laboratory was eventually built in 1945 many of the big old timbers from the barn were used in the construction, especially for the foundation.

The first building to be erected on Orgonon was a one-room cottage, completed in 1943. It had a large, built-in desk—practically the only furniture in the cabin—and was used by Reich solely for his writing. The log cabin on Mooselookmeguntic Lake consisted of one large room, with two little bedrooms attached to it as an afterthought, as it were, so that all social activity took place in that one central room. This was not very conducive to writing or to concentration on difficult problems. Whenever Reich needed to be alone he withdrew to the cabin at Orgonon about six miles away. This cabin was enlarged in 1945 with another room and a kitchen, and further additions were put up in 1948 when the caretaker and his family moved in for a number of years.

Mr. Templeton, the old Maine guide who had built the original log cabin, remained a friend of Reich's and took care of the cabin during the winter months. He had developed cancer and had to have an operation. Reich talked to him about the accumulator with the suggestion that it might help alleviate some pain. Templeton was eager to try it, and built one for himself which he used regularly under Reich's supervision. He became so interested in it that he eventually took over the building of these apparatus, and soon they were being shipped out from Maine. His daughter helped him, and after his death early in 1944 she continued the work until 1947, when a local building contractor took over. By that time there were approximately thirty accumulators in use. The War Production Board had issued a permit to the Orgone Institute Research Laboratories, Inc. so that the necessary sheet iron for the accumulators could be purchased.

When the Orgonon property was acquired, Reich was very excited about it, and he began to dream about the potentials of the place. He had a big sheet of plywood on which he painted a map of the research center as he envisioned it. It was a beautiful vision, and he was determined, with his usual enthusiasm, to make it come true. He saw experimental laboratories, research hospitals and treatment centers, a central library, a children's center, study halls, residence houses for researchers' and physicians' families, a telescope observatory with a sliding dome. He kept his dream for more than ten years, and was able to eventually realize part of it. Later on he managed to arouse enough enthusiasm in some of his co-workers to make it appear as if more of these plans could be realized, but no one was able to sustain this enthusiasm long enough—or to make the necessary sacrifices—to make Reich's vision come true. In the years to come Reich would walk again and again over the property, carrying little wooden markers and designating the spots where he saw the buildings in his mind.

During 1943 Reich had worked on mathematical equations for his concepts and had arrived at what he called an orgonometric equation which was the key to his biophysical functionalism. He wanted to establish his priority in this field, and in March 1944 he deposited this equation and a statement regarding his discoveries with friends of his work in various parts of the world. In a letter that accompanied these documents he said that the knowledge and the techniques contained in his discoveries gave him great power which he was ready to use against those who were not willing to help secure human liberty and decency, even if it meant that they might put him in jail or hang him. We can surmise from this letter that he felt the discovery of orgone energy held potentials of such magnitude that if they were developed into practical applications it would mean great political power—which he would be willing to use for bringing about desirable social changes.

Although Reich chided Neill about the importance of world recognition, he was very pleased—and wrote to his friends about it—when in 1944 his name appeared both in the *World Almanac* and in *American Men of Science*. I have often wondered about his clinging to these straws of official recognition despite his denial of their having any real value. There can be little doubt that there was a basic feeling of insecurity in Reich. It manifested itself in another way that I observed on many occasions. As I have mentioned, Reich gave himself completely naturally, and with great patience and gentleness to his patients, and he was the same way with children. But if a stranger called for an appointment, a new trainee coming for a first interview, for example, Reich always went through the same routine: a *mise-en-scène,* as it were, playing the great scientist. It always amused me, though I would not have dared mention it. He would be in his study, deeply engrossed in writing, wearing a freshly laundered laboratory coat. He would give his visitor the impression that he did him a great favor by interrupting such important work to see him. Reich was an impressive figure, and I am sure that most of his visitors were awed by their first interview.

In spite of the fact that Reich began to earn a fair amount during the early forties with his psychiatric work with trainees, we continued to live on a very modest scale. By far the larger part of his earnings went into the Orgone Research Fund to be used for research work. Salaries had to be paid, new instruments bought and constructed, and Orgonon built up; there was not much money left for private use. We had a cleaning woman for the house, but I did the shopping and cooking. Reich's own requirements were not extensive. He liked to be well dressed when he went out, and had two or three very good suits, but for work he usually wore khaki pants, an open shirt without tie, a wool or tweed jacket, and the inevitable laboratory coat—special ones downstairs for lab work, and others upstairs for psychotherapy.

Reich drank moderately during those years. He liked a highball before and after dinner, and a good wine with his meal when we ate at a restaurant. But he smoked heavily, at least two packs of cigarettes a day. He thought, and said so whenever I worried about his smoking too much, that if one breathes well smoking does no harm. But it was in those years that he began to suffer from frequent attacks of tachycardia with pulse rates up to 240 beats per minute, lasting from four to twenty-four hours, and he developed coughing paroxysms that often ended in short but complete blackouts. He also became much more worried about and conscious of his skin disease. In Scandinavia he had gone swimming and bathing with his friends, but he now allowed only his family to be with him. Our social life became more and more restricted; we saw very few people socially, and certainly did not entertain. We still went to concerts occasionally, and took Sunday drives into the country. Eva, who was a college student, came to see us fairly frequently. Reich had hoped at one point that she might come and live with us, and had arranged for one of the top-floor rooms to be at her disposal, but this hope did not materialize. She was still too ambivalent, and too much torn between her parents. Lore had more or less withdrawn from contact with her father, and came to see us very seldom.

One change in our life occurred in April 1944 with the birth of our son Peter. Reich was absolutely delighted with the child, although the baby upset our work schedule quite a bit. Reich had been very worried for days before the birth that we would not make it to the hospital in time, that there would be a snowstorm and we would not get through. Of course, everything went smoothly. I was very grateful to have him with me during most of my labor because he was so gentle and understanding. The doctor who attended me had been a co-student of Reich's in Vienna, and the two of them went out to celebrate the birth of Reich's first son with a big bottle of champagne.

Reich wrote to Neill about the discoveries he was now making into the real nature of the newborn. He wrote that after twenty-five years of psychiatry, he felt almost like a new student of psychology watching the baby. He thought that these observations made it clear that our views on education were 100 per cent wrong; for instance, he noticed that a three-months-old baby is not autistic, but wants to participate, if only with his eyes, in his environment. I would like to quote directly from one of his letters because I feel it is pertinent in view of the fact that today, twenty-three years later, Reich's son is serving in the U.S. Army. On May 2, 1944, Reich said: "I can only hope that we shall at least succeed in making the next war happen not within the next twenty-five years, but after the next fifty years, so that this boy won't have to die for liberty, but will be able to live and work for liberty."

One subject we rarely had any argument or difference of opinion about was the upbringing of the child. And if there was a difference of opinion, we were always able to discuss it openly and rationally and settle it to Peter's benefit, even after our separation and until Reich's death. I think we both consciously tried not to use the child for our own purposes, not to use him as an extension of our own egos, but rather loved him as an independent being, watched over his growth together, and tried to protect him from harm. I have the feeling that Reich had become aware of the fact that he had pressured his older daughter too much to follow his ideas, and now he tried to avoid a repetition with his son. He succeeded in this except for the last two years of his life when the pressure on him became so crushing that he sometimes forgot Peter was only a child.

When I said that we lived on a very modest scale, I really meant it. We bought for the baby's room secondhand furniture which I repainted in my spare time. At the same time, Reich bought a new X-ray machine to investigate the energy field phenomena; he spent thousands of dollars on it. It was always the same—the work came first, family second, but I did not mind at all and it did not even occur to me to object.

After a while Reich found that the baby took more of my time than he had anticipated. He felt that he needed my work more than the child needed me, and therefore we started to employ a full-time maid. I was very lucky to be able, in the early years of the child's growing up, to combine my work with my function as a mother. Because everything was under one roof, I could thus satisfy the demands made on me by father and by son.

During 1944 Reich continued his studies into the problems of work democracy. Reich had coined the phrase "work democracy" as a contrast to political democracy. He understood in that concept the working together of all life necessary forces in their factual functioning for the benefit of mankind. It was not the political power of an office that was important. A person should have the right to make decisions affecting work processes only in the realm in which he actually performed his work—physicians to decide on the medical needs of the population, builders to decide on housing and construction needs, garbage men to decide on the collection and disposal of garbage, et cetera. He saw an interaction on the national and international level of people working in the same field, and an interaction between all life-necessary work to function as government on the national level. He definitely wanted government. He once said to one of his students in regard to anarchism: "We don't want anarchy, we want order. We take the rational core from anarchism and communism. I have great admiration for Kropotkin. But they forget that times change, that yesterday's truth is today's lie."

He tried to apply the work-democratic principle—that a person should have the right to make decisions affecting work processes only in the realm in which he actually performs work—to the structure of his own organization. There would be no formal officers, no presidents or other administrators making decisions about the research or the use of funds. Only those who did the work would have the right to speak up and make decisions.

That same year he worked on the seemingly insoluble question of why the human animal was unable to acknowledge the sexual basis of the many ills that plagued it. I remember that he read to me once a short article, which I think was never published, in which he described a society where the sexual taboos were replaced by the same taboos regarding eating. It was a rather horrible parallel, and I guess he felt that it was hitting too deeply to be generally acceptable.

We moved back to our cabin on Mooselookmeguntic Lake in Maine at the end of June 1944 with the baby and with Eva accompanying us for a few weeks. Several impressions of that summer have stayed with me, because they were so typical both of our way of life and of Reich. I had to continue my work, which at that time and place consisted mainly of typing Reich's manuscripts. I also had to take care of the baby. I remember well typing away at a manuscript while pushing the carriage back and forth with one foot to keep the baby quiet because Daddy could not bear to hear him cry. Or Reich, very graciously telling me in the late afternoon to take off for a while and go fishing out on the lake while he would look after the baby—then, after half an hour, his waving to me frantically because the baby needed to be changed, an ordeal which he could not face.

There was in late August the threat of a hurricane passing over our region. Reich had always had a deep fear of being trapped by natural forces beyond his control, such as thunderstorms, fires, or windstorms. He was always prepared to fight his way out, if necessary, during the very heavy thunderstorms that we often experienced in the Rangeley region. He would get dressed if the storm occurred during the night, and have a pail of water or sand and an axe handy. He prepared for the hurricane in the same way, and when the heavy storm started he insisted that the baby in his cradle be placed under the very heavy table in case the roof should be smashed by falling trees. It is true we did lose a few trees in that storm, one missing our cabin by just a few inches.

I also remember our walking over the grounds of Orgonon many afternoons, through the back fields, up the hill to a spot at the edge of the woods overlooking lakes and mountains. We carried Peter in a hammock between us. This was one of Reich's favorite spots and he often mentioned that he wanted to be buried there.

Reich was very much involved, as I have mentioned before, in measuring the energy fields of all living matter. He was excited about his success in building an energy-field meter that would react only to biological energy. For instance, if a person approached this meter it would register that person's field, and there were different fields for different people; it would also show a reaction to a living plant but not to a dead stick. Most of the articles Reich wrote about the biophysical areas of his work were first published in the *International Journal*. A translation of the German *Character Analysis* ably done by Dr. Wolfe was issued by Orgone Institute Press in 1945. A sociologist student of Reich's pressed for an English edition of *Mass Psychology,* and Wolfe now started work on this translation. I remember him, always carrying his little attaché case, coming for endless evening discussions about the correct phrasing of a paragraph here, the right word for one of Reich's special expressions there, and I always admired the conscientiousness with which Wolfe was able to convey the exact meaning of Reich's concepts.

Wolfe's ability to immerse himself completely in Reich's ideas and theories is evident from his translations. The role Wolfe played in Reich's work in the forties has, I feel, never been enough emphasized. It was his devotion and unending effort that made a success of Orgone Institute Press. He acted for years as a sounding board for any new venture. Wolfe had a brilliant, discerning, and critical mind, but he still was not immune to Reich's criticism. Everybody had to "be creative," had to "produce," and I now think that Wolfe must have felt hounded by these incessant demands of Reich. Wolfe was first and foremost a psychiatrist and like many before and after him he was unwilling to follow Reich into fields where he felt he was not sufficiently trained or competent to follow. Although it never came to a complete break between the two, Wolfe withdrew more and more from active participation at the beginning of the fifties—a withdrawal dictated also by prolonged illness.

At the end of the war, international contacts were renewed and expanded. In 1944 a small number of interested physicists and psy-

chologists in England had started a study group in the field of
orgone energy phenomena and planned to send one of their participants for study with Reich. In Israel, the psychiatrist Dr. Walter
Hoppe had built a few accumulators and had embarked on experimental orgone therapy. Others in Israel were busy with translations
of some of Reich's books and articles. Contact with the Scandinavian friends was re-established, and Dr. Raknes made plans for a
study trip to the United States.

The need for a place where many could study became obvious, a
place that would accommodate a large number of students who
wished to observe the energy phenomena, to learn the Reich blood
test for detection of cancer and general biopathies, to study the
effects of orgone energy application on cancer in mice, to follow
the development of protozoa and bions under the microscope. In
the summer of 1945 the so-called Student Laboratory was constructed near the site of the old barn. It had a very large main hall
for the microscopic work, facilities for the biological preparations,
a mouse room, and a special room—completely encased with sheet
iron and equipped with many specially constructed instruments—
for the observation of orgone energy. It was a very beautiful place
to work, with large windows overlooking the mountains and lakes,
and it was to be the center of summer conferences, lectures, and
courses for many years.

Reich's interest in the development of the baby continued to
grow. He wrote Neill in 1945 that he wanted to escape from the
world of the neurotic and give all his time to investigating living
matter. He thought that our only hope for a saner world lay with
newborn babies. His interest in the sex-economic upbringing of
children led in the fall of 1945 to a seminar on the newborn child
with pediatricians, educators, and social workers. It was a lively
group, and the lectures and discussions were extremely interesting
and thought-provoking. A small nursery school started in 1944 by
one of Reich's students contributed much material to this seminar.

The experimental work both with cancer patients and the biophysical aspects of orgone energy continued undiminished throughout the year. In the *International Journal* in 1945 appeared the
first article by Reich on the Emotional Plague—his term for life-
negative, irrational reactions that appear in personal and social
interrelationships. The term was originally intended to describe

a neurotic symptom of a certain character structure. "Plaguey" later became a sort of derogatory catchall term used by many of Reich's self-styled defenders to label anyone who did not fully agree with all of Reich's actions.

On May 28, 1946, after a very extensive and long hearing, Reich became a United States citizen. His dossier was thick, but the hearing was conducted in a pleasant and considerate manner. Since it had taken place over a few hours, and the stenographer was not too sure that she had always understood correctly, the interrogating official suggested that Reich come back and read the transcript of the interview before it was forwarded to Washington. When Reich did so a few days later, he found only one mistake that very definitely needed correction. When asked about his memberships in various organizations, Reich had mentioned among others the International Society for Plasmogeny which had become, in the words of the stenographer, the International Society for Polygamy—not a very salutary association for a future citizen!

That same year Reich received an honorary membership in the Mark Twain Society, and he took it as a great honor to a good citizen—raising the old question of recognition again. He wrote about this new honor to Neill, mentioning all the important names on the letterhead, such as Eisenhower and Winston Churchill. I always had the feeling that these memberships were quite routine matters, awarded to anyone who publishes a book or becomes connected with an educational institution. But Reich took it as personal recognition. He was very naïve and very European when it came to American honorary memberships. However he did wonder whether the officials of the Mark Twain Society really knew what he was doing. He thought that his work with orgone energy was more dangerous than sex-economy. Sex-economy, he said, dealt only with moral issues, while orgone energy, the cosmic energy, touched on God.

Reich expected both positive and negative reactions to his work from the world, and he began in 1946 to work on his *Rede an den kleinen Mann* (Talk to the Little Man). This was intended, in the beginning, as a private rebuttal to the many adversities, the stupid annoyances that had to be dealt with and made it necessary for him to interrupt his work. It was not intended for publication. Most of Reich's close co-workers and friends were impressed by the manuscript, but advised against publication. The decision to publish it two years later came only after the many unpleasant and slanderous articles on Reich appeared in 1947.

In the summer of 1946 the first laboratory course was held at Orgonon. The English group had sent a young psychology student to study with Reich and work in the laboratory; some of the social workers and educators ran a small children's camp near Rangeley where our son Peter went during the day; a few of the physicians in training with Reich came for a few weeks to work and study in the laboratory. The entire staff moved from Forest Hills to Orgonon during the summer, living in Rangeley and nearby camps. The Reich family moved to the small cabin at Orgonon to be closer to the work. It was rather primitive living; the water had to be brought from the spring in pails, and we had to take our showers in the laboratory washroom. But it was not for very long. During June and July a small house for the family was being built, a bit farther away from the laboratory but still on Orgonon. We settled there by the end of August. The house, known as The Lower Cabin, became our permanent home in Maine from then on.

The young English student who was at Orgonon during July and August was to figure in the debate between Reich and Neill on criticism. The subject of criticism had come up earlier in connection with Dr. Tage Philipson, the Danish psychiatrist who, after the war, had criticized some of Reich's new developments of character-analytic therapy without having studied them firsthand. Now this young Englishman came and started to criticize. I shall not forget his first day at Orgonon. He arrived late in the afternoon, unannounced. I met him by chance on the road to the Students' Laboratory, at which time he demanded to see Reich immediately. I told him that I did not think Reich would see him, but that I would try. I called Reich on the interphone from the laboratory, and he agreed to see the new arrival for a few minutes while I tried to arrange for his accommodations. I sent him down to the cabin, and as Reich told me later, the young man entered and without further ado started to criticize, saying that on pages so and so in your book *The Function of the Orgasm* you said something with which I absolutely disagree. He kept on enumerating other pages in other books with which he did not agree. I am still surprised that Reich did not throw him out. Neill once said that he did not understand why Reich got so involved with those people who were so *unbedeutend* (insignificant) to his work. But it was the whole concept of criticism that was in question for Reich, not the individual instance. To Reich criticism was valid only if based on thorough investigation culminating in similar or other conclusions. He felt that most criticism was based on a neurotic need for self-assertion. A student had first to learn to listen *unvoreingenommen* (unprejudiced) before working at a given task and thereby earning the right to criticize.

People often said the Reich was not able to take criticism, although he always invited it. I think he was willing to listen if he felt that a person knew what he was talking about and was sincerely trying to help the work rather than simply insisting on self-assertion.

In September 1946 Dr. Raknes came to the States for four months. He spent the first month working with Reich in the laboratory at Orgonon, staying at a camp nearby. He later returned to New York with us, living near us in Forest Hills.

The only publication of Orgone Institute Press that appeared in that year was the English edition of the *Mass Psychology of Fascism*. It had been revised and enlarged, and thus differed from the 1933 German edition. Reich had to eliminate many of those phrases that had been written under the influence of political ideology. He had to revise especially his appraisal of the Soviet sexual revolution which was becoming more and more reactionary under Stalin's regime. He added to this English edition three of his major articles on his concept of work-democracy that had previously been published in the *International Journal*. The journal was suspended during 1946 and replaced by the *Annals of the Orgone Institute* in 1947.

The year 1947 brought several important events, both positive and negative. On the positive side was a growing following for Reich's work, a visit from Neill, and a grand celebration of Reich's fiftieth birthday. On the negative side, difficulties in our personal lives, a vicious campaign in major magazines and newspapers against Reich's work, and a resultant investigation by the Food and Drug Administration.

Psychiatrists came in large numbers to be trained by Reich, to satisfy the growing demand among many lay-people for orgone therapists. Reich feared that the popularity of orgone therapy would mean a corruption of its principles, and he complained that the increased needs of his work resulting from the growing demand forced him to ask for fees that made him feel like an exploiter. But he had said, before coming to the United States, that he was not afraid of getting involved in the American money-making ways because he would use any money he made for constructive purposes—which is exactly what he did. The growing expenses of the experimental work took up whatever money he was making. The discovery of a motor force in orgone energy, for instance, necessitated at that time the purchase and construction of new and expensive instruments.

Neill's first visit to the United States was divided between a lecture tour beginning with a seminar at the Hamilton School in Sheffield, Massachusetts for teachers and social workers, and a visit of several weeks at Orgonon. Neill and Reich talked deep into the night over a glass of whiskey and innumerable cigarettes. All their favorite topics were taken up: criticism, recognition, socialism, communism, sex-economy in pedagogy, and especially the newborn child, as Neill had recently become the father of a little girl and found this experience, as did Reich, a marvelous field of study. They also discussed the United States. Reich had become a great American patriot. He insisted that no European could understand that Roosevelt's government had done more for the working class in the United States than had any socialist government in Europe. He insisted that the socialists in Europe had spread the misconception that education in the United States was backward; Reich found conservative Americans more open-minded and progressive in matters of living and education than the rabid European socialists.

Neill saw some of the experimental work that was going on at Orgonon, but he maintained that he did not really understand it. While Neill was at Orgonon, one of his former teachers who had gone to Canada came for a visit and showed so much interest in the accumulators that he became for a while the builder and distributor of accumulators in Canada. One incident that Neill remembers very clearly is that one afternoon, during which we all sat together talking about cars and other mundane matters, Reich told Neill that such drawing-room conversations about nothing were sheer agony for him, they took him out of his sphere of thinking and he could not participate. This was always true for Reich, and was mentioned as a part of his character by many others to whom I talked. He could not and would not participate in chitchat and small talk.

One exception to Reich's boredom with light-hearted affairs was a reception held on March 24 at Forest Hills in honor of Reich's fiftieth birthday. It was an open house for friends, co-workers, and students, and Reich enjoyed it very much. He was usually conscious of important dates, always remembering birthdays of his family. He loved to give and receive flowers on these occasions, especially pink carnations. The only holiday which he liked to celebrate was New Year. We often dressed more or less formally on that occasion, even if alone at home, and celebrated with a good dinner and a bottle of champagne. Reich always summarized in his diary on New Year's Eve the important events of the year. It was his habit to send short, personal New Year's greetings to his friends and co-workers. He did not like commercial greeting cards, and never used them.

In the early spring of 1947, our son Peter started going to nursery school. The work with crayons and colors now fascinated him to the extent that he began making his drawings all over the house. Reich very patiently explained to the child that the house belonged to all of us, that people came to see Daddy and to work with him, and that therefore the part of the house where we worked could not be used for his drawings. He was free to use his own room and no one would interfere. We had the room painted completely with oil paint, gave Peter water colors and finger paints that could easily be washed off the walls, and he went to work eagerly.

When we returned to Forest Hills in the fall, Neill came with us for about two weeks, giving a few lectures in the New York region. I remember one afternoon when Peter asked his father and Neill to make some paintings on his wall. Both men started to paint happily—Neill drawing a big red cat, and Reich, at Peter's express wish, a red fire engine. Neill's cat stayed up for quite a while, but the fire engine eventually gave way to the Lone Ranger.

I think the small incident of Peter's newly acquired passion for painting clarifies how Reich felt about the difference between freedom and license. Letting the child paint all over the house would have been license. But showing Peter that his freedom to paint was restricted by the freedom of others to have their part of the house clear of his paintings gave the child a practical example of how freedom involves responsibility toward others. Reich's principle of self-regulation for the child has so often been misinterpreted to mean complete and unrestricted freedom—or rather license—that one cannot emphasize enough the real meaning of this concept.

In April and May of 1947 I took my first vacation away from all my duties and went to England to visit my mother and brother. Reich had urged me to take a vacation, and after long discussions over whether to leave the child with him or take him along, we decided to leave him in Forest Hills. We had very competent household help at that time. Reich was a bit afraid of handling the child by himself—and even paid me a great compliment by admitting that I was definitely much better with the child than he was. We thought that with the postwar conditions in England, with rationing still very much in effect, the child would be better off at home. I sailed on the *Queen Elizabeth* on the memorable trip when she got stuck for two days on a sandbank outside Southampton harbor. Newsreels and newspapers were full of stories about it, but the passengers were not allowed to send reassuring cables to their families for twelve hours. I was told upon my return that when Reich heard the story over the radio, he paced the floor like a caged lion, full of his usual anxiety about the safety of others, and had the secretary ring the Cunard Line for news every half hour.

When I came back, however, Reich put me through a third-degree questioning as to everyone I had seen in England. He asked especially whether I had been faithful to him during these two months. I almost had to take an oath of fidelity before he would be satisfied. Of course I knew about his jealousy, but I found at that time a moralistic attitude in him such as he usually attacked in others. The double standard of sexual behavior was quite apparent in his attack. I was not allowed to question his faithfulness to me during that period, but I was quite certain that he did not apply to himself the same standards that he expected of me. In fact I knew that he had had an affair although he didn't tell me so.

Although he always preached that sexual behavior cannot be judged by moral standards but only by standards of health or sickness, he was not entirely free of moral judgments of sexuality. His following a double standard in regard to sexual behavior of wife and husband was one contradiction, the other was his attitude toward homosexuality. He never knowingly accepted a homosexual for treatment. Dr. Havrevold told me, during the interview in Oslo in 1966, that he once tried to refer a very worthy professional man to Reich for training, but when Reich heard that the person was a homosexual he not only refused to accept him, but said, *"Ich will mit solchen Schweinereien nichts zu tun haben."* (I don't want to deal with such filth.) In a letter to Neill early in 1948 this attitude came to the fore again when Reich described the difference between sex-economy and sexology as it was represented by the World League for Sex-Reform and similar organizations. He wrote that sex-economy dealt with the problems of natural genitality, while sexology concentrated on Indian phalli, condoms, and homosexual perversions. This moralistic attitude toward homosexuality is, to my mind, another aspect of some unresolved conflicts in Reich's own character structure.

Political animosity, sensationalism, and fear of competition must have played a role in the attacks against Reich's work that began that year with an article published in *Harper's Magazine* of April 1947 by the free-lance writer Mildred Edie Brady under the title "The New Cult of Sex and Anarchy." The same writer followed with another article in the *New Republic* of May 26, 1947, titled "The Strange Case of Wilhelm Reich." These articles, containing truths, half-truths, outright lies, and vicious insinuations became the source of innumerable other articles in both reputable and not so reputable periodicals for years to come. It seems that not one of the article writers ever bothered to check facts by examining Reich's own writings, but took Brady's articles as the gospel truth, to be spread with further embellishments in the cause of pornography and sensationalism.

Mrs. Brady had obtained an interview with Reich under false pretenses, saying that she was bringing greetings from friends on the West Coast. She had been told by Reich that he did not want publicity, and that he was not in the habit of giving interviews. But that did not deter her from going ahead with her attack. The entire story of Mrs. Brady and the "American Campaign" was written up by Dr. Wolfe in 1948 under the title "The Emotional Plague versus Orgone Biophysics," published by Orgone Institute Press. I would agree with Dr. Wolfe that no doubt there were some communists involved in this campaign, and that the perpetrators received encouragement from psychiatric and psychoanalytic circles. There may have been a concerted effort to stop the spreading of Reich's work. But I, personally, do not believe in a Moscow-directed conspiracy, as claimed by Reich.

As a result of the Brady articles the Food and Drug Administration started their investigation of the orgone accumulators.

I was there in the summer of 1947 when an inspector of the FDA appeared at Orgonon, mentioning the Brady article as the inspiration of the investigation. Throughout the following years this investigation continued. It eventually culminated in the injunction against the distribution of accumulators and the court trials of 1956 and 1957. In spite of the fact that Reich and his co-workers had published both positive and negative results obtained with the accumulators; in spite of the fact that no responsible physician ever mentioned a cure for anything in connection with the accumulator; in spite of the fact that it was clearly stated again and again that here was an experimental device to be used only on an experimental basis; and in spite of the ridiculously small number of accumulators ever in use, no more than about three hundred in all—in spite of all these easily verified facts, the accumulator was presented by sensationalist articles and by the FDA as being promoted as a cure-all, as a device for "enhancing sexual potency." In their investigations over the years, in interviews with co-workers of the institute, and with physicians and patients, they kept the idea of a sexual racket connected with Orgonon and the orgone accumulator in the foreground at all times, and always based their charges on the insinuations published by the sensationalist press.

Aside from Dr. Wolfe's reply to these attacks, and some letters to the editors of various magazines and periodicals written by co-workers, nothing was done. Reich did not feel that one could gain much by prolonging arguments with these partially hidden and underhanded attackers, and his lawyer agreed that nothing could be gained by a libel suit. It was a waste of time that could be used better in positive work, and so, on the whole, one ignored the attacks and concentrated on the task at hand. Reich said at that time that it was not what people thought of him but what he did that counted.

The first number of the *Annals of the Orgone Institute* appeared in 1947. A second summer course at Orgonon took place, mostly on laboratory techniques with bions, protozoa, and the blood test. And plans formed for an international conference in 1948, and for the building of an Orgone Energy Observatory on the hill at Orgonon.

There is no doubt that by 1947 there was much public and scientific interest in Reich's work in general, and especially in orgone therapy. The literature had been spreading slowly and steadily, but until the slanderous attacks there had been very little publicity about Reich's work in the general press.

In the winter of 1947–1948, the number of trainees was mounting and occupied Reich for several hours every day, while the biological and biophysical laboratory experiments continued to intensify.

Reich no longer liked to go into the city for concerts or plays, but went with pleasure to the local movie houses once or twice a week, to the beach, and out for dinner once in a while. Peter reminded me of one such occasion, when we went for dinner sometime in April 1948 to the restaurant in Forest Hills that had become *the* restaurant for us, and where we were quite well known. The child had just received as a birthday present a complete Hopalong Cassidy outfit—black shirt and pants, black cowboy boots and hat, and a two-gun holster set—and he would not be separated from any of it during the meal. The orchestra began a beautiful Viennese waltz and Reich wanted to dance, but I was reluctant to leave the child alone at the table. Whereupon Reich led the child up to the orchestra stand and sat him down on the steps. Peter remembers sitting proudly there in his beautiful outfit, watching his parents dance the Viennese waltz. I think it must have been the last time that we danced in a public place.

During the early months of 1948, Reich worked with an architect on the plans for the Orgone Energy Observatory. As soon as the ground was free from frost, a local contractor began to lay the foundations. We moved back to Rangeley in May, and all laboratory work was transferred to Orgonon at that time. In

March of that year Reich had experimented with Geiger counters and with vacuum tubes, and had made several important discoveries about the behavior of orgone energy.

He had also started to experiment with a small motor moved by orgone energy. This work continued in Maine with the help of a young assistant who concentrated on the elaboration of these phenomena. Reich was very excited about the reactions of the little motor. Notes kept by some students at the laboratory, and put at my disposal as source material, mention the work with the motor again and again as one of Reich's preoccupations that summer. He knew that a great deal of work was needed to "clean" the experiment, to clarify all its ramifications and functions because, as he put it, it sometimes behaved like "an hysterical woman." Reich foresaw a great future for his orgone-energy motor.

We planned the First International Orgonomic Convention for the summer of 1948. Reich invited a Norwegian photographer, Kari Berggrav, who had worked with him in the laboratory in Oslo and who was now living in the United States. She came to Orgonon that summer to help with making various films. Before the convention started, Reich wanted an outdoor film showing Orgonon in its regional setting. Among a student's notes I found the following observation that seems so typical of Reich's eagerness and involvement in any task. He had hired Kari, a professional photographer, but he would rarely let her do the work. As the student put it: "He didn't let Kari, whom he calls his photographic expert, *be* his photographic expert."

There were films made of the various experiments with vacuum tubes, Geiger counters, and the Orgone Energy Motor, and some of people working in the laboratory. Reich told Kari to have a big title before the latter pictures, saying WORK, underlined, with two exclamation points, and then wondered whether to make the title rather WORK, NOT POLITICS, referring to his work-democratic concepts.

It was just before the convention started, during the work period that summer in the Students' Laboratory, that Reich had a number of posters printed with one of his favorite slogans—IT CAN BE DONE—which were placed in strategic spots in the laboratory, somewhat reminiscent of IBM's THINK posters.

Shortly after our arrival in Maine, preparations began. Invitations were mailed. Some of the foreign participants needed a written invitation in order to obtain the necessary visa for the trip.

Besides the continuing experimental work, Reich began to write his paper on orgonomic functionalism which he presented in a series of lectures during the convention in August. It established his philosophical basis for the orgone energy concept, which he elaborated in his book *Ether, God and Devil,* published as the second volume of the *Annals of the Orgone Institute* in 1949.

Many of the physicians who had been trained over the past seven years by Reich began to give lectures on orgone research, the concept of self-regulation, psychiatric orgone therapy, and other related subjects. Reich enjoyed all these activities and the growth of his work. In a February 1948 letter to Neill, in continuation of their never-ending controversy about recognition, he wrote, "you underestimate the recognition I enjoy in the world."

For the first orgonomic convention Neill returned to Orgonon, this time with his wife and child. Dr. Walter Hoppe came from Israel, Dr. Ferrari from Argentina, Dr. Raknes from Norway. For some unexplained reason, Dr. Hoppe was taken to Ellis Island upon his arrival at the airport in New York on August 28. He was not released until August 30, after the sum of five hundred dollars had been deposited with the Immigration Service. Reich was unbelievably, frighteningly furious about this persecution of his work. He sent telegrams to the State Department, the Justice Department, to Ellis Island, and to his lawyer Arthur Garfield Hays. One of our young assistants of that summer, a medical student, remembers some of the things Reich said at the time. "This is research," he kept saying. "He cures their cancers and they throw him in jail." Or, "This is research, young medical student, not just something for sitting and thinking about. This is part of your education, not just a little incident."

Eventually Dr. Hoppe arrived by seaplane from Portland, landed on Dodge Pond at our little swimming dock, and was welcomed by all participants of the conference with such emotion that it must have made up for the anguish of the previous days.

There were thirty-five participants—physicians, educators, laboratory assistants. Reich gave his lectures on orgonomic functionalism; there were demonstrations in the laboratory of the biophysical experiments with orgone energy, and films that had been taken in the laboratory were shown. The participants from foreign countries reported on their activities in the field of orgonomy. Reich also talked about the concept of the emotional plague. He emphasized especially that to him this was a neurotic symptom that manifests itself in socially harmful actions, and that it should not be used for name-calling. Another important aspect of this concept which Reich stressed time and again during the conference was the need to fight the plague wherever it appeared, to safeguard the newborn child from the emotionally crippling effects of that plague, and to work for the untouchable life principle in children.

It was in one of the conference lectures that Reich proposed to change the name of his therapy from Vegetotherapy to Orgone Therapy, and there were discussions on how much of the physical orgone therapy (with the accumulator) was to be incorporated into the psychiatric orgone therapy. The recurring themes in all of Reich's talks during the summer conference were the human fear of all new discoveries, and the difference between traditional science (which thinks of phenomena as static, absolute, and resting, which talks about the empty space) and orgonomy, the new science which thinks about space filled with a basic, primordial, moving energy.

With the many people swarming around Orgonon that summer, there were quite a few social activities going on. Reich did not participate much in these. One reception for all participants was held in the Students' Laboratory at the beginning of the conference. The Neills stayed with us, Dr. Raknes and Dr. Hoppe were occasional dinner guests at our house, and some of the others were asked on and off for afternoon tea or a drink, but this was the extent of Reich's participation in the social life. I attended with Peter some of the parties given by various participants for their co-workers and their families, but Reich would not let me go with most of the younger people to the weekly square dances in the village, much to my regret. He thought that close social intercourse by him and his family with his trainees and students would lead to contempt on their part, and he insisted that I maintain only a more or less formal contact with them.

Reich's daughter Eva was one of the participants at the conference. She was engrossed in her medical studies and interested in her father's work, although still a bit afraid to enter into it fully.

A sad misunderstanding earlier in the year had widened the rift between Reich and his younger daughter Lore. Early that year Reich had undergone a series of painful tooth extractions, and it was on one of the days when he was in pain, and so swollen-jawed that he was unable to talk to anyone, that Lore, who happened to be in the neighborhood, decided to come and see him. She told me years later that it had cost her a great deal to make that decision after years of separation, and yet, when she finally came, Reich would not see her. She did not accept or understand the reason for it—a mere toothache—and felt rejected by him. But Reich was rather vain, and especially after not having seen Lore for a few years, could not face her with a swollen jaw and while unable to speak. Lore did not renew the contact for quite a few years; we did then meet her husband once or twice, but there was no real relationship between Reich and Lore from then on.

During the summer months of 1948, the observatory on the hill kept growing. Since it was intended in future times to carry a heavy telescope, the foundation was laid on solid rock. The entire building was constructed of fieldstone, with walls twenty to twenty-four inches thick. The man who was over the years caretaker of the property, Thomas Ross, had become to Reich and our family not only an employee but a trusted friend and co-worker. He had grown up on that land and remembered where his grandfather used to deposit stones plowed up from the soil. This was a great help in locating suitable material for the walls and fireplaces of the observatory. Reich was deeply involved with the building process. He watched the daily progress and admired the skill of the workers; he was especially fascinated with the work of the stonemasons—their almost intuitive knowledge of which stone to place where. The workmen responded to his interest and appreciation of their work. I think they felt that to him there was no status difference between the workman and the scholar so long as each man did his work with the skill and the knowledge of his profession. A warm relationship developed between them. Reich talked with some about their families and children, and to this day some of them have kept a warm, friendly, and loyal feeling toward him.

During 1947 Wolfe had translated the manuscript of the talk to the little man, and Reich had shown it to several friends and colleagues, among them the cartoonist William Steig. Steig felt that the text called for illustrations that would bring the spirit of the accusations even closer to the reader. Although many friends, among them Neill, felt that the book should not be published, Reich himself needed to blast at the world after the attacks in the press and by the various professional organizations against his work. And the addition of the Steig illustrations seemed to make it more acceptable. Thus, *Listen, Little Man!* was published by Orgone Institute Press in 1948. It received a mixed reaction from the national press, but some of the cartoons were impressive enough so that they were used with their captions from the book on ashtrays and highball glasses.

The second volume of *The Discovery of the Orgone: The Cancer Biopathy* was also published in 1948. It contained many articles that had appeared in the *International Journal* between 1942 and 1945 regarding the biophysical aspects of orgone energy and its functioning in the human body. It stated Reich's concept of the origin and development of what he called the carcinomatous shrinking biopathy. It was a theoretical, scientific elaboration of these concepts, difficult to read and to understand for anyone not trained in thinking in functional terms, but it was most certainly not a "promotion of a cancer cure" as it was labeled later by people who had not read or understood it.

By the end of 1948 it became obvious that a concerted effort was being made by the American Psychiatric Association against the spreading of psychiatric orgone therapy. Several psychiatrists who had been trained by Reich and had begun to practice psychiatric orgone therapy were dismissed from the staffs of hospitals where they worked after their refusal to give up a therapy which they thought beneficial to their patients. Others were denied promotions in professional associations. Still others, in private practice, were approached by the A.P.A. and advised to sever their connection with Reich. All these men, graduates of medical schools of high standing and respected members of professional organizations, had come to find in orgone therapy a better way of helping their patients—and on that basis preferred to sever their connections with the established medical associations rather than with Reich. Reports came to the Orgone Institute that in lectures and courses given by members of the American Psychiatric Association and the New York Psychoanalytic Association derogatory remarks about Reich and orgone therapy crept in again and again; and rumors made the rounds that Reich was in a mental hospital.

In order to put up a united front against these attacks on Reich and orgone therapy by the established medical organizations, twenty-three physicians practicing orgone therapy formed the American Association for Medical Orgonomy. This organization, like all others in Reich's orbit, was established on work-democratic principles. No formal titles were given, no directors elected; only those who worked actively in the field and did the work in the organization could determine the functions of the association. I have in my files a copy of a letter which I wrote on December 9, 1948, to Neill in which I talked about my worries about these attacks and happenings. It may shed additional light on the situation as it was through my reaction to it at the time.

Here is some additional, private information on the situation. We have talked about it over and over again with most of the physicians, privately and in meetings. I think the greatest fault we made was in not fighting immediately, years ago, the rumor about Reich's schizophrenia. Since it was never denied and fought against, people who did not know what was behind it all just took it as the truth, and it is now used in lectures in psychiatric institutions where it is always brought up in connection with *Characteranalysis*. They invariably say that Reich was brilliant and O.K. up to 1934, but that he deteriorated after that and is now schizophrenic. They try to scare young psychiatrists who are dissatisfied with their methods from coming to Reich for training, and they don't even shy from blackmailing people. So many reports about such incidents are coming in, that there can be no doubt that it is a concerted action. Our lawyer advises strongly now doing something before it grows completely out of our hands. It seems sometimes as if it were so already. It is a nasty situation, takes up all our time and the Stimmung [mood] is accordingly.

A big meeting [twenty physicians] last week decided unanimously for forming immediately an Association for Medical Orgone Therapy, since they all felt themselves in a much better position to fight if they were an organized body instead of each one fighting individually. I think it is a very good thing, especially as all concerned are fully aware of the dangers of "organization." But people being what they are (cowards), they need to be organized to get up enough courage to fight. And they will have to fight. There are a few good people amongst them and maybe we shall get somewhere.

The good reports that come in are encouraging, the books continue to sell, the younger psychiatrists are eager for lectures (but are afraid of the strong organizations which are against Reich), people like Godwin Watson come out more and more strongly in the sexual question for adolescents. But we somehow cannot enjoy all this as much as we are depressed by the continuous attacks.

Do you remember the two psychoanalysts, Brodsky and Finger, who came up to the lab at Orgonon one day, talked to Ferrari and me, and then came back the next day to talk to you? Well, Brodsky, according to the latest report, is just preparing an article for the *Psychoanalytic Journal,* saying that he saw it all, and that the whole Orgone theory is a completely schizophrenic idea, and paranoic system. What can you do about that? If they come and we keep them out and don't show them anything, they say we are hiding something mysterious, and if you show it to them who know nothing about it, and they don't understand it, then it is schizophrenic. But they would not take the trouble to study it or even to try to understand the practical results. It sometimes seems hopeless and it is no consolation to hear again and again from well-meaning people that this is the way all geniuses have been persecuted all through history.

I am sorry to trouble you with all this, but it is a relief to me that I can write to you frankly, about this whole mess.

As we drove back to Forest Hills late in the fall of 1948, we were coming around a rather sharp curve on one of the not-too-wide Maine roads, when a fully loaded lumber truck came toward us on the wrong side of the road. Reich pulled sharply over, blowing his horn so furiously and with such force that it broke. It was a horn that was like a narrow wheel fitted inside the steering wheel, and it remained broken as long as we had the car.

Reich was a very careful and conscientious driver, always watching the cars in front and behind, glaring ferociously at anyone who did not abide by the rules of the road. Often he would pull over and stop to let a car that followed too closely for his taste pass by while he fixed the driver with a very stern look. He usually gave his passengers a running commentary, dwelling on the killer instinct in most drivers. When I first started to drive in this country, Reich would sit next to me repeating over and over "keep to the right," so that I heard his "keep to the right, keep to the right," in my head for weeks after he finally permitted me to drive alone.

Reich worked hard the winter of 1948–1949, training more physicians and writing. He worked on the orgonometric equations which were to be published in the *Orgone Energy Bulletin* in 1950 and 1951. He wrote an extensive case history about orgone therapy with schizophrenia, and prepared a paper on the "Expressive Language of the Living." Both papers were included in the third, enlarged edition of *Character Analysis* published in 1949.

In February he had several severe attacks of tachycardia, and several blackouts from coughing paroxysms. He decided to cut down on his excessive smoking, but did not succeed too well with his resolve. He did not feel that his physical symptoms were the result of overwork. He thought rather that they were due to a fear that his efforts would be lost through misuse, misinterpretation, or degeneration. He wrote to Neill that it was not the overwork that ate him up, but the danger that he might give up in despair. During a three-day attack of tachycardia, I succeeded in having him consult a physician who was reassuring but insisted that one could do nothing to slow down the pulse rate. I think that was about the last time Reich of his own free will consulted a heart specialist.

Reich promised to take a vacation. It consisted of going back to Maine in May the long way around, via Vermont and New Hampshire, doing the trip in three days instead of one. And of course the moment we were at Orgonon the work started again —his own work, and also the aggravations we had come to expect in connection with the building of the observatory. Reich had arranged with the contractor not for an overall, fixed price for the building, but rather for a pay-as-you-go arrangement with monthly bills accounting for materials and labor, to be kept within the limits of the estimate. For all of us who worked in any capacity at the office and laboratory during 1948 and 1949 while the building was going up, the day the bill came was sheer agony. We all tried to avoid Reich as much as possible on that day. He would wave the bill around—especially at me as I was the bookkeeper—shouting about all the extras that were in the bill and needed to be checked. I had to spend hours and hours examining every single item on the bill and double-checking all extras. I have a feeling that the few mistakes I found were not worth my time and effort, and most definitely were not worth the unnecessary aggravation they added to Reich's strenuous activities. But he was convinced that this was the only way of keeping the contractor to his estimated figures.

Reich had another worry that summer. The young assistant who had helped him with the development of the orgone energy motor and his orgonometric equations, and who was supposed to spend another summer at Orgonon, had disappeared together with the motor. He had been introduced to Reich by one of our assistants who had met him as a fellow student at the University of Chicago. Inquiries after his disappearance both at Chicago and other institutions where he had presumably worked disclosed that he had never been matriculated but had been just an auditor. He was even unknown at some places. There was no doubt in the mind of anyone who had worked with him that he was a brilliant mathematician with a very good background in physics; but the young man was unreliable.

Reich developed a theory which he maintained all through the following years that the young man had been kidnapped by communist conspirators who wanted the secret of the motor force in orgone energy, and who wished to steal the priority of the orgonometric equations. We have never had a satisfactory explanation of the young man's disappearance. The assistant who introduced him to the work felt that the high-pressure intellectual atmosphere around Reich had become too much for the young man, and he thus had dropped out and away as did so many others before and after him. Some co-workers seemed to agree with Reich's theory of a communist-inspired conspiracy. My opinion—not supported by any fact but just by my observation of the young man—has always been that he probably spent some time in a mental institution at that period and didn't want the fact to be known. Everybody speculated with some pet theory regarding the disappearance, but nobody undertook any serious search for the young man.

That summer, so many of the physicians trained by Reich showed an interest in the laboratory course on the cancer problem that two courses were given. Reich gave the theoretical lectures, and several of the laboratory assistants, including myself, gave instruction in the Reich blood test and other laboratory techniques, such as the preparation of bions. During these courses so much enthusiasm was generated about the possibilities of establishing a treatment center that it appeared as if Reich's vision of 1943 for an Orgone Research Hospital and Treatment Center might come true. Plans were drawn up for a center, the site at Orgonon staked out, and a road bulldozed to the site. Reich was enthusiastic and contemplated remaining at Orgonon for the winter as a first step in the development of an Orgonomic University. He planned to have the hospital functioning by 1952. But as I have indicated before, few were able to attain his degree of enthusiasm, and still fewer were willing to make the same sacrifices, personal and financial. The plans came to nought, and in the end Reich was again let down.

The observatory building was finished in early August. Reich moved into his study, workrooms, and laboratory. The main activity continued in the Students' Laboratory, but some of Reich's special instruments—microscopes, oscillographs, Geiger counters —were transferred to the large, first-floor laboratory hall.

At the same time, the sculptress Jo Jenks came to make a bust of Reich. She had been in touch with Orgonomy for many years. Reich was a great admirer of Jo's work, and had a small reproduction of her "Rock Woman" in his study. The work on the bust progressed rapidly. Jo told me that Reich did not talk much about himself during the sittings, but rather went on about the plans for future developments. After the sittings were finished Reich wrote a letter to Jo in which he talked about what a great experience participation in such creative work was for him, and how it felt to see a work of art grow out of an inner emotional expression. He felt that such creative work went to the core of the life problem, to its very depth.

Other visitors that summer included again Reich's daughter Eva who was drawing closer and closer to his work. The Hamiltons, both of them educators who had been in training with Reich and who were trying to run their farm school on the principles of self-regulation, came with their children for a brief visit. In September two Sundays were set aside for an open house at the Observatory so that people in the Rangeley region would have an opportunity to see the house, the instruments, and the work facilities, to dispel any speculation about mysterious goings-on at Orgonon. I believe that more than two hundred people took advantage of this opportunity.

We still thought that we might spend the winter in Maine, and some of the physicians connected with the work continued to come up from the New York area every weekend for a course with Reich—quite an undertaking considering that the various turnpikes and throughways had not been completed and the trip took anywhere from twelve to fourteen hours. I think they finally succeeded in persuading him that it would be much easier for all concerned if he were to return to New York. Reich agreed with this, especially since he was afraid of losing touch with human problems. He wanted to develop his orgonometry and his equations without the disturbing influence of the world of the neurotic; but as pleasant as it was to sit in his ivory tower—or stone castle—at Orgonon, the unifying concept of orgone energy would not permit him to separate the purely theoretical aspects of orgone energy functions from the practical application of the same energy functions to the human being, whether in psychiatric orgone therapy or in biophysical orgone therapy with the accumulator.

In November we returned to Forest Hills where Reich continued his course for the physicians on Clinical Demonstration of Medical Orgonomy and started another series of lectures in line with his always burning interest in infants.

The second international orgonomic conference was being prepared for the summer of 1950. Special lectures and a special day were planned on the subject of the healthy child.

Interest in Reich's work kept growing in the United States and elsewhere. There was a great deal of correspondence with scientists and other interested people abroad, reports kept coming in from study groups containing details on experimental work done in England, Denmark, Switzerland, and Italy.

Reich's old fascination with the story of Christ received new impetus at that time, and he read every book that he could find on the subject. He was laying the foundation for his *Murder of Christ.*

By the end of 1949 a step had been taken, especially with the planned expansion at Orgonon, toward the establishment of a Maine-based organization. Thus the Wilhelm Reich Foundation was incorporated as a nonprofit research and educational corporation in the State of Maine. It provided the roof under which the various components of orgonomy could be gathered. It embraced Reich's own theoretical and experimental work at Orgonon, as well as an Orgonomic Research Clinic in Forest Hills, an Orgonomic Children's Clinic in New York, the publications of Orgone Institute Press, and the Orgonomic Infant Research Center in Forest Hills.

Reich visualized the foundation in the image of a clinic with a responsible head and assistants functioning in a work-democratic way. He did not want a dictatorship. The actual function of a worker was to determine his participation in administration. No one was to be elected to an office unless he actually fulfilled the work of that office, to begin with. There were to be no nominal titles and offices.

In January of 1950, in connection with the clinical lectures on medical orgonomy, the Orgone Institute Diagnostic Clinic was started in Forest Hills under Reich's direction. The main purpose of this weekly clinic was to screen candidates for training in orgone therapy and refer patients either for orgone therapy or to general psychiatric clinics. The diagnostic clinic was later combined with the Orgone Energy Clinic, also in Forest Hills, where Reich blood tests and other tests were given for early diagnosis of cancer and other biopathies.

The Orgonomic Infant Research Center was established as an outgrowth of Reich's lectures on the healthy child. It was to become the center for study of the healthy child from prenatal development through adolescence. Plans to coordinate a children's center at Orgonon with a hospital and treatment center were discussed, and Reich approached Neill with the proposal that he assume the directorship of such an orgonomic children's center. But Neill refused. He felt that such a step would make him into a disciple, and he preferred his independence and friendship with Reich to a discipleship.

Although Reich thrived on the activities at Forest Hills that winter of 1949–1950, we decided to move permanently to Maine in the spring of 1950. One of the reasons, though not a decisive one, was that our son had reached school age and the constant shifting from one school to another was not good for him. We both felt that for the first few years of schooling the elementary school of

Rangeley was more desirable than a city school, and Peter, who had attended the subprimary grade in Rangeley from September through November, had liked it much better than the private school near us in Forest Hills. Early in 1950 most of our furniture, equipment, and personal belongings, including the library, were packed off and moved to Orgonon. The building in Forest Hills continued to function as a clinic until 1952, when the house was sold.

The summer work in Maine started again with cancer courses and ended with the Second Orgonomic Conference in which about fifty-five people participated. There were that summer several well-trained biologists studying with Reich. The summer is described well in a letter one of them wrote to a friend.

I came to Rangeley the last week in June and remained until September 1st. It was a tremendous experience. . . . Reich was at a workbench; he got up and came across the floor in a charge of energy and I knew that his glance as we shook hands took me in from head to toe. We sat down at the business table to talk about my work program which was to include daily use of the accumulator and darkroom. . . . I was almost immediately aware that Reich was a very dynamic and very much alive individual. . . . Reich's methodology [is] also very good; he insisted that I observe everything that was going on. This gave me a good opportunity to get the feel of the place and the people. . . . At first I had a difficult enough time, because I tried to either prove or disprove things. Eventually I think that I did learn that only the observable facts are important and not my peculiarly distorted ideas about these facts. . . . Cancer course: Reich proved to be as dynamic a teacher as he is a person —a tremendous help in presenting his concepts of the basic functional relationship between cancer cells and protozoa—that cancer cells are protozoa, or amoeboid-like cells which break loose in the body, and begin to function in an independent manner. . . . II. International Orgonomic Conference—definite highlight of the summer. . . .

The Conference was again an international gathering, but it was dampened for many of us by the fact that the U.S. Consulate in London had denied a visa to Neill. In spite of efforts by many interested people there was such a prolonged delay that Neill finally gave up. What it was that brought about the delay could not be clearly established, but it seems that Neill in one of his books had made the remark that he was basically a communist, and although to my knowledge he never belonged to the Communist Party or to any party, that one statement was enough to make his status as a visitor questionable. It kept him away from the States from then on, and although their correspondence continued until Reich's imprisonment, the two friends did not meet again. Neill told me that after Reich's death he could have come to the United States on several occasions. But he could not face it. He said that Reich's death had left such a blank, that it would not have been the same.

At the convention, which was again preceded by a reception in the students' laboratory for all participants, there were reports given by the visitors from abroad and by the heads of the various departments of the foundation. Dr. Raknes gave a lengthy report on activities in Scandinavia and it was good for Reich to hear that some of his former colleagues were still actively interested and functioning in sex-economic work, among them foremost Dr. Nic Waal in Denmark and Norway. Reich reported on the work in the Orgonomic Infant Research Center in his lecture "Children of the Future," and discussed his theoretical work with orgonometric equations. Neill's paper on sex-economic pedagogy was read.

After the conference we slowly settled down for the winter's work in Maine. Besides our family, quite a few others had decided to stay on. The orgone therapist Dr. Simeon Tropp bought a house in Rangeley where he established his family. Dr. Helen MacDonald, a biologist from California, settled in a small house in Rangeley. Several others rented apartments in the town, among them Eva Reich who had just finished her medical studies, and one of Reich's assistants, Myron Sharaf. The activities of the Orgone Institute Press were transferred to Rangeley and the business manager, Lois Wyvell, also settled there. Another young physician-in-training and his wife decided to spend the winter in Rangeley, and there were altogether about eight professional workers sharing in the winter work. Some of them had specific programs on one or another aspect of Reich's work. Dr. MacDonald planned the standardization of Reich's Experiment XX which dealt with problems of biogenesis, and Dr. Tropp was working on a project concerning the influence of orgone energy on hereditary cancer in mice. Reich himself made plans for the ORANUR experiment. It was Reich's idea to help mankind eradicate the terrible effects of the atom bomb through a three-fold attack: by using orgone energy to heal radiation sickness, to neutralize the effect of an atom bomb, and, eventually, to immunize mankind against nuclear radiation. I lack the scientific background to give a detailed theoretical explanation of this experiment, and must refer interested readers to the report *The Oranur Experiment,* published by the Wilhelm Reich Foundation in 1951. Copies may not be easily available since they were part of the material burned or otherwise destroyed by the U.S. government in 1956.

Before the winter work began, Reich decided to take a brief vacation, and just the two of us went for about ten days at the end of October 1950 to Southwest Harbor on Mount Desert Island in Maine. We stayed for once in a good hotel and there we spent the last really peaceful days of our marriage. It was the quiet before a storm—for the storm broke that winter and never fully abated for Reich, although many new discoveries and developments were still to come.

There was another attack based on rumor—not too serious, but a nuisance. During the summer months, the children's camp near Rangeley had again been in operation, though not directly connected with Orgonon or the foundation. We had thought that the various investigations by the Food and Drug Administration and other government agencies had been laid to rest, and were therefore quite surprised when a counselor at the camp was interrogated by an FBI agent concerning slanderous statements of a sexual nature made in the town about Orgonon and the camp. After we had protested to the FBI office in Boston, we were informed that they had not sent an investigator to Rangeley to interview anyone, and we never learned who in fact that investigator was. At the same time, our lawyer informed us that an official of the Maine State Police had told him that complaints about Orgonon had been found to be completely without basis, that the FBI had cleared Reich of any suspicions regarding his political status, and that the people in Rangeley in general spoke highly of the work done at Orgonon.

Such nuisance interferences kept on creeping up, taking time away from more important work. Still, no one at that time had an inkling that the investigation of the accumulator by the Food and Drug Administration was still under way.

There is no doubt that quite a few people in Rangeley were suspicious of the many outsiders who now came to live in their midst. The local people did not and could not really understand the work done at Orgonon and were suspicious of it. For example, the wife of one of the physicians who had planned to spend the winter in Rangeley was a well-trained teacher; when she applied locally for a teaching position she was told straight away by the superintendent of schools that no one connected with Orgonon could expect a job in the Rangeley schools.

After our vacation, the family settled in the observatory for the winter. I have to confess that I never liked living in the observatory, and that I always felt unhappy when I had to live there. It was all right for working, but it had never been intended for family living. There was no room where one could sit down for a meal—the kitchen was too small for that and all the other rooms were work rooms—so we put up a table in the laboratory hall. There was no room for the child. He either had to sleep on the enclosed porch outside Reich's study or in one of the two rooms that had been added to the basement as maid's rooms—pleasant enough, but out of hearing distance and difficult to reach through the furnace room. My bedroom was a cheerful room with its own bath, but it was isolated from the rest of the house. The family was thus dispersed over the huge building. Except for Reich's study with the large fireplace there was really no place to meet as a family and be comfortable; if Reich were in the middle of a problem there he could not tolerate anyone around him. But there was nothing to be done about it, because at that period the lower cabin was not prepared for winter living.

Even with his helpful and eager workers around him, Reich felt very much alone. He wrote to Neill in November 1950 that he was basically alone, that there were very few close workers who really understood what he was doing—he mentioned Dr. Baker and Dr. Wolfe among those who did—that he felt pessimistic, that he would have to forget the present and think in terms of a thousand years hence. Although the circle of co-workers was small and working well together, Reich kept himself aloof from any intimate contact. He saw Dr. Tropp on a more personal basis on and off, and of course Eva spent a good deal of time with us during those winter months. I remember the Thanksgiving Dinner that year, carefully planned for our little community and in which we all were to participate; Reich, at the last minute, refused to come.

Peter started school and, after encountering some difficulties as an outsider in the beginning, soon settled down happily with a number of friends. Some of his friends who went regularly to Sunday School at one of the local churches invited Peter to come along. He went and came home with a beautiful picture of God with a long beard sitting amidst clouds and angels. Peter asked his father whether this God was a real person. Reich explained to Peter that there was no such person, that God was all around us and in us, in anything that is good and living, like the orgone energy he knew about. During this period Reich was very much preoccupied with the Christ story and he had talked in the family group on many occasions about Jesus. Peter now asked whether Jesus was a real person and Reich said yes, Jesus had been a real person, a good teacher and a wonderful man. So, when one day in school some of the children asked Peter whether he believed in God, Peter to their great surprise answered that no, he did not believe in God, but when further questioned whether he believed in Jesus, his answer was yes, of course, Jesus was a real person and he believed in him. Thus, Peter became an acceptable member of the community, and his good standing in his group was absolutely assured.

This was the background against which our winter work began. Over the years, the atmospheric observations with the electroscope had continued and Reich felt he had ascertained certain techniques of weather prediction that seemed to be working much better than the established methods. He was interested in the formation and the paths of hurricanes, and he used the experience gathered in those years in his later "cloudbusting" experiments. (Reich always felt the need to use special terminology for his discoveries and for each new development, which often added to the difficulties of understanding the already difficult material.) In November of 1950 he made some observations during a hurricane-like storm which he found so important that he incorporated them in preliminary research reports, published in the *Orgone Energy Bulletin* in April 1951.

Since 1948, Reich had kept certain government agencies, especially the Atomic Energy Commission, informed about his discoveries with orgone energy—about the reactions obtained in the vacuum tubes, and the motor force. Reich had on several occasions indicated that the experimental work with orgone energy demanded much more than the private means at his disposal. Time and again he had received polite answers that work with orgone energy was outside the scope of the Atomic Energy Commission. Now, before entering upon the Oranur Experiment, he again got in touch with the AEC, advising them of his intentions and trying to find out whether there were any restrictions on his work. He received the answer that no one at the AEC would be able to pass judgment on orgone energy experiments, and thus there were no restrictions on his work. Reich was able to obtain the necessary radioisotopes for the experiment.

I cannot go into the intricate theory and technical aspects of the experiment here. But all through the period of the experiment itself, from December 15, 1950, through March 1951 (although the aftermath of the experiment continued for many more years), Reich kept a steady stream of letters and information going to those government offices that he felt needed to be informed on the progress of the work. In his book *The Oranur Experiment,* published in 1951, Reich has given an extensive account of the biophysical and biological results of the experiment. Although, as we shall see, the first results were rather tragic—in the way they affected the health of most people involved and in the way they turned Reich's expectations into a disaster—Reich felt that in the final analysis the solution might yet be found through an immunization process.

U.S.A.: 1951–1956

The first series of experiments with radiation was started on December 15, 1950. These experiments were divided more or less into two approaches to the same phenomenon. One was the physical measurement with Geiger counters and electroscopes, the other was observation of biological reactions in mice. Reich's expectations, based on his theory and previous experiments, were that orgone energy in high concentration would neutralize nuclear energy, and that the mice which had been exposed to nuclear energy in the form of radium needles would not develop radiation sickness if immediately treated with orgone energy. But his expectations were completely overturned. As he explained it, instead of neutralizing nuclear energy, the highly concentrated orgone got ever more excited, the Geiger counters ran absolutely wild, and counts were at times so high that the apparatus jammed. According to Reich, the very small amount of radioactive material employed in these experiments could not explain the incredibly high counts he obtained, and he therefore ascribed them to orgone energy reaction to the radioactive material. All of us who worked in the laboratory in those weeks were immediately affected in one way or another by nausea, conjunctivitis, and general malaise, and the students' laboratory was more or less evacuated, no one staying in there for more than three to five minutes at a time. Much of the microscopic work had to be transferred to the Observatory or to the living quarters of the assistants.

The trouble began to show itself in early February. Originally, all laboratory assistants took turns taking care of the mice on Sundays. It was my turn Sunday, February 11, and I had a terrible shock when I opened one after another of those boxes containing mice in the Oranur Experiment, and counted about forty dead test animals. I alerted Reich and the other assistants, and all through that Sunday we dissected these mice and found in all of them the same symptoms of radiation sickness. It was a most upsetting experience to all of us, but it was by far not the end of events set into motion by the Oranur Experiment. I think that by the end of that year every one of us who was involved in that experiment had reacted not only with physical symptoms, but with equally strong emotional upsets. A few of the assistants had to leave Orgonon early in the spring of 1951, among them Eva who had suffered a severe attack of radiation sickness and could not stand the atmosphere at Orgonon either physically or emotionally. I became seriously ill at the end of March with some of the symptoms attributable to radiation exposure. An operation became necessary, and I was away from Orgonon for six weeks. The work in general was very much curtailed, and the prospect for summer courses and conferences was dim.

Before these frightening events, however, and even during the beginning of that unpleasant period, we all enjoyed the winter in Rangeley to a certain extent. There were beautiful, sunny days, deep snow, and we did quite a bit of skiing, although Reich who once had been an ardent skier now went rather carefully about it, skiing just on the gentle slopes of Orgonon. I have a feeling that he was more aware of his heart condition than he would admit, and he was probably very wise in not overexerting himself. His physical reaction to the Oranur experiment came later than most, in October of that year, conditioned by his exposure to the contaminated atmosphere and by emotional distress over the outcome of this experiment. He had a very severe heart attack and was in bed for six weeks. He said at that time that every heart disease is really a heartbreak disease. There is no doubt that the outcome of the Oranur experiment contributed to his heartbreak.

One activity that broke out in Reich, as he put it, in reaction to the Oranur Experiment—as his way of fighting his personal Oranur sickness as it were—was painting. He painted furiously, ten pictures in two weeks, large oil canvasses. He continued his painting whenever he was at Orgonon. His pictures have a very definite character, use brilliant colors, and I find them very fascinating not as great art but as a characteristic expression of the man Reich. As I have indicated before, there was much influence of Munch in color and choice of subjects. Reich was very much intrigued by the fact that we cannot really reproduce some of the color and light we see around us. The light of the sun on leaves, on water, on the clouds, and on flowers was a challenging subject for him, as was the image of the flames in a fire, and he painted these subjects over and over again. He wrote in a letter to Neill in June 1951, "If *art* is a disease, Oranur has brought out the artist in me. . . . I just enjoy painting tremendously. It teaches me a lot about our miserable failure to see nature correctly. It is incredible to detect that you do not know how sunlight hits a tree, and that there is no color to render in true fashion the color of sun and daylight. . . . I am also playing and enjoying the organ, and have begun to write down melodies of which I am quite full."

Reich continued his work on the Oranur Experiment, trying to learn what had gone wrong, trying to turn it into a positive experience. He had hopes that eventually a process of immunization could be realized, perhaps by public agencies, for the benefit of mankind. Like so many of Reich's discoveries, this Oranur Experiment may be taken up again some day in the future, with the results hopefully to be used in the way he wanted them to be used.

Just a few days before Reich had his heart attack, he wrote a long letter to Neill which shows the agonies he suffered in those

1. Reich's mother, Cecile Reich, neé Roniger. The handwriting at the top of the photograph is Wilhelm Reich's.

2. Reich's father, Leon Reich.

3. Reich in the field as lieutenant in the Austrian Army, 1917.

4. A formal portrait of Reich, 1921.

Members of the Psychoanalytic Polyclinic in Vienna, 1922. (Fourth from the left, *t row, the director of the clinic, Dr. E. Hitschmann; next to him W. Reich, and on the right, Dr. Annie Reich.)*

6. *Wilhelm and Annie Reich with Eva and Lore, summer 1928.*

7. *Above left: Reich in Maine, summer 1942.*

8. *Above right: Wilhelm, Ilse, and Peter Reich in Maine, summer 1944.*

9. *Left: Reich and his son Peter, Maine, summer 1945.*

10. *Right: At work in the laboratory at Orgonon, 1947.*

11. *Below: Reich explaining the functioning of the orgone motor during the summer conference of 1948 at Orgonon Students' Laboratory. At left, Dr. T. P. Wolfe.*

12. *A field at Orgonon with marker for a future building.*

13. *Reich and Neill at Orgonon, summer 1947.*

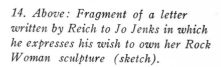

14. *Above: Fragment of a letter written by Reich to Jo Jenks in which he expresses his wish to own her Rock Woman sculpture (sketch).*

Above: Jo Jenks at work on Reich's [bust], Orgonon Observatory, summer [194]8.

16. *Right: Sculpture of woman by Jo Jenks that Reich wanted to purchase.*

17, 18, 19. *The three photographs on this page show the different, often contradictory sides of Reich as time passed. At above left, Reich in Maine, summer 1941. Above right, again in Maine, summer 1945. Below, Reich in 1953.*

weeks. In this letter of October 7, 1951, he tries to explain why people call him a dictator. They want him to approve of their misuse of his work and cannot take it when he objects to this misuse. He blames these people for forcing him to destroy one organization after another because its work grew the wrong way. He complains that in order to keep his work clean he had to give up recognition and much needed human contacts. He talks about the way people remain sitting and then blame him when they cannot follow his moving onward. As he puts it, "I did not change away from my line of twenty years ago, I only pursued it further." He mentions the large numbers of his books being sold all over the world, and points out that the awareness of his discovery becomes ever more acute.

It is a letter full of contradiction, despair about mankind, and self-reassurance that recognition of his accomplishments is growing.

In spite of the many interruptions and the disorganization, certain aspects of the work continued to function. People continued to come for training with Reich, and he started to write the *Murder of Christ* which had long been in preparation. Orgone Institute Press continued that year with the publication of the *Orgone Energy Bulletin* containing, among others, articles by Reich about the cancer cells in Experiment XX, his orgonometric equations, orgonomic interpretation of the dowsing phenomenon, and one article about his studies of newborn infants. Besides these bulletins, two books by Reich were also published that year by Orgone Institute Press—the two volumes on orgonomic functionalism, *Ether, God and Devil,* and *Cosmic Superimposition;* the latter Reich gave me when it appeared in November with the inscription, "During the period of Do or Die." Reich's booklet on the Orgone Energy Accumulator appeared that year too.

No courses were given and no conferences held during the summer months because prolonged work in the students' laboratory had become impossible. Most of the work was carried on in the observatory, and it was a comparatively peaceful summer. There was one official interference at the Canadian border but it was more nuisance than anything too serious. A Canadian biologist who came regularly for weekend study and training with Reich was suddenly one day detained by the U.S. Customs office and

asked questions about his own and Reich's political beliefs. Insinuations were made about some kind of sex racket at Orgonon.
Reich, very much incensed about this, sent a letter of complaint
to the president's office in Washington. There may have been some
reaction to it, because the next time this biologist crossed the
border he not only did not encounter any difficulties, but he recalls
that the man who had questioned him before practically hid when
he saw the car approaching. Perhaps some reprimand had come
from a higher authority.

The difficulties were not only in the general situation at Orgonon; they also affected my relationship to Reich. As I have indicated before, when the outside world seemed threatening Reich's
wrath turned against those closest to him. I had suffered severely
—both physically and emotionally—from the Oranur effect, and
I was frightened. I was also disturbed by the insecurity of our
living conditions. When Reich added to this his completely irrational accusations about my supposed infidelities, life became too
difficult and our relationship started to deteriorate. Neither of us
was willing to give up what we had built over the past twelve years
and we both tried to make a go of it, but it became increasingly
more strenuous. Moreover, I was less and less able to follow Reich
in the development of his work, and as life with Reich was the
equivalent of life with Reich's work, this contributed to our drawing apart.

One of the few joys Reich had in those trying years was his
relationship with our son Peter. We lived during the summer
months in the lower cabin, and worked in the observatory. Reich
would continue to work there by himself after all others had
stopped work in the early afternoon. Usually around five o'clock, he
would fire two rifle shots as a signal to Peter that he was ready
for him, and Peter would race up to the observatory. He either
had a talk with Daddy, or they would listen together to the radio
or look at television, or, best of all, they would go for a walk
through the back fields and woods of Orgonon. They would come
back happy and hungry for dinner. Peter remembers these walks
and talks with his father very distinctly as an important part of
his growing up. The relationship between the two was always close
and very good. Reich was usually very gentle with the boy, and
I can remember only two occasions when Reich was really angry

with him. Once, when Peter was about four years old, he played with matches—one of the very few taboos imposed on him—and almost set the house on fire. Reich was very angry and gave the child a hard slap. Knowing Reich's fear of fire, especially in the woods, this was not surprising.

The only other incident that I remember when Reich slapped Peter had to do with Reich's almost fanatical demands for the truth in all and every situation. Peter was accused of having taken candy from another child, and he denied it. But the candy was sticking out of his pocket, and Reich punished him severely—not for taking the candy, but for lying.

In October 1951 Reich had a very severe heart attack, and although it was suggested by those physicians who were at Orgonon at that time that he might be better taken care of in a hospital or that he should at least have an oxygen tent at his disposal or that he should see a heart specialist, he absolutely refused, and insisted on curing himself with orgone therapy; but he gave up smoking for good. I took care of him in the beginning, but he became increasingly suspicious of my good will and during the last two weeks of his convalescence had his daughter Eva come back to take care of him.

After Reich's recovery the family settled again for the winter in the observatory, with other co-workers continuing to live in Rangeley; we stayed there until March. It was a busy winter, and things seemed to smooth out a bit. Some of the orgone therapists from the New York area came more or less regularly once or twice a month for conferences with Reich. I think it was that year that Reich decided to give a Christmas gift to some of his closer co-workers and ordered several copies of one of his favorite books to be sent to them. This was an English translation of De Coster's *Tyl Ulenspiegel* with woodcuts by Frans Masereel. Whenever the old question of "the ten books one would take to a desert island" came up, this book was always among Reich's choices, along with Nietzsche's *Also Sprach Zarathustra,* and the Bible. Another book which according to Reich belonged in every library was F. A. Lange's *History of Materialism.* All through the fourteen years of our marriage, the fact that I had never been able to study this last book was a frequent bone of contention.

During the summer months Reich had written up the *Oranur*

Experiment, and he continued now his work on *Murder of Christ* and *People in Trouble.* The work with mice had been discontinued, but the labaratory work on Experiment XX and atmospheric measurements went forward. In March of 1952 Reich started on a new phase of orgonomy which I have never been able to follow or understand. Reich put me under great pressure to "see" many of the phenomena he discovered at the time, but I have always doubted my subjective impressions. I cannot judge this work in any way, since I did not participate in it. I concentrated my activities during the period from March 1952 until my separation from Reich in August 1954 on the administrative end of the work, on coordinating the various efforts of the foundation. I translated important correspondence—for instance Reich's correspondence with Freud, in which task Myron Sharaf collaborated with me—and gathered together, put in sequential order, and typed the bibliography on orgonomy which was eventually published by Orgone Institute Press in 1953 as *Wilhelm Reich, Biographical Material, History of the Discovery of the Life Energy, European and American Period, 1920–1952.*

The new phase, the cosmic orgone engineering (CORE), dealt not only with cosmic phenomena, outer space, and space ships, but with weather conditions, droughts, and rain-making. It started with Reich's discovery of the "blackening of the rocks," of deadly orgone energy (DOR) in the atmosphere, and with his efforts to remove this deadly orgone with the help of "cloudbusters" which were also used in his rainmaking efforts.

I think now that Reich may again have been ahead of his contemporaries in noticing a disturbance in the atmospheric conditions and its effect on the population. What he so dramatically called DOR or deadly orgone energy, and ascribed to interference created in outer space as part of an attack on Earth, is to my thinking probably the same phenomenon that was in the 1960's recognized universally as air pollution created by man himself in this technological age. (Hopefully, Reich's cloudbuster or DOR-buster principles may yet be utilized in the future so they can serve as a weapon in the fight against this serious threat to man's environment.)

The cloudbuster was an arrangement of hollow pipes placed on a sort of turntable that could be manipulated to point in any desired direction. The pipes were connected to cables which had to be put into the ground or into a source of water, preferably flowing water. The theory behind it was that the pipes would draw the orgone energy from the clouds, and that the water in turn would draw the collected orgone energy out of the pipes and neutralize its effect, especially if it were a concentration of DOR. At other times, cloud formation was to be triggered by means of the cloudbuster, as prolonged pointing in a given direction would theoretically give rise to a stronger concentration of the energy in the otherwise more-or-less uniform energy envelope of the earth. Thus, the cloudbuster was meant to function in the destruction and in the formation of clouds. The entire CORE project was an attempt at a practical application of Reich's theory of energy-filled space, of our living in an orgone-energy ocean.

Reich, in *Orgone Energy Bulletin,* Vol. VI, published in July 1954, described the function of the cloudbuster as being based on the principle of the lightning rod, but controlling orgone energy rather than electrical energy.

The literature published by Orgone Institute Press contains many volumes on this research work under the CORE name, and I have to leave it to scientific investigators to evaluate the various aspects of this work. I shall concentrate here only on the work's consequences on human relationships, and reactions to this work and to Reich by his co-workers and assistants.

First of all, in March 1952 Orgonon was evacuated because of the DOR situation. Reich never stayed more than two days in the same place at Orgonon; he traveled around the region, sometimes sleeping in a hotel, sometimes in a tent. Peter and I lived in a small apartment in the village, and eventually moved with Reich into Dr. Tropp's house in Rangeley when he and his family left for a prolonged vacation away from Oranur, DOR, and Orgonon, It was a time of intense restlessness. The purely physical conditions of living were absolutely impossible. Reich went back to the observatory on several occasions, suffered blackouts, and once fell asleep there for several hours and looked severely ill and almost in shock when he finally got out.

Again, Reich probably was not too sure of his own theories and observations, and therefore demanded from all of his assistants absolute identification with the work. Very few of us were able to do this. Looking back, I think one had to be either a genius or an artist trained in visual observations to distinguish the nuances and variations in the color of rocks, in the shape of the clouds. They were mostly subjective impressions, and although there were objective factors involved, Reich often saw these phenomena first on a subjective basis, and expected others to see the same things. And if you were not a genius or not an artist, then you either followed blindly or withdrew from the work.

Reich's assistant Myron Sharaf was among those who could not follow. Sharaf tried to explain to Neill, who was worried and puzzled about what was happening at Orgonon, why he had left Orgonon in May 1952. I would like to quote from his letter.

> . . . The nature of orgonomy and Reich's nature (which is to my mind pretty much identical with orgonomy at its very deepest) are so terribly challenging, complex, and demanding that you can't just "be yourself" with them as you can almost anywhere else. . . . Reich certainly encouraged independent efforts [but] he expected too much and we wanted desperately to live up to his expectations. . . . The clearest thing to me is the difference in functioning between Reich and others, and the effect "genius" has on ordinariness when the two are in immediate contact with each other. . . .

Sharaf went on to say in that letter that no one blamed Reich for what had happened with Oranur, that Reich was very considerate in helping everyone to take precautions and in giving time to those who were ill. He also wrote that many left because Reich was moving into an area where they could not follow; they wanted to develop that particular part of the knowledge already gained in their work with Reich and in which they wanted to function.

By the end of July, Reich thought that it was safe for us to move back to the lower cabin.

Reich had constructed by that time the first cloudbuster apparatus, and was anxious to put it to work. He continued during the summer with the cloudbusting experiments, and local newspapers sometimes noted that he was successful on several occasions in breaking prolonged drought situations.

We received that summer another hint that the Food and Drug Administration was still investigating the accumulators. Three FDA inspectors drove to Orgonon at the end of July and barged in unannounced, ignoring signs that indicated clearly that no one was allowed to drive up to the Observatory without previous appointment. Since these inspectors did not have any papers authorizing their visit, Reich refused to see them and ordered them to leave the property.

The observatory building was still not usable for any length of time, and Reich felt that we should make plans to move to Rangeley for the winter. He was still traveling around a great deal, measuring the various atmospheric conditions, watching the blackening of the rocks, and working with the cloudbuster on DOR removal. In September 1952 he had ordered two cloudbusters built to his specifications by a factory in Portland, Maine. He now used them in several foglifting, DOR-removal, and rainmaking operations during the late summer and fall of 1952. Several of the orgone therapists in the New York area became involved in the DOR situation and began using cloudbuster methods to clean the air of pollution. Reich believed, on the basis of his experiments, that a small, strong accumulator connected with pipes to a source of running water would draw the DOR from the body, working on the same principle as the cloudbuster, and a small DOR accumulator was used by some physicians in their medical practices.

In the fall of 1952 Peter and I moved into the little house in Rangeley that belonged to Dr. Helen MacDonald, who had gone back to California. Reich lived in various places, sometimes spending days on end with us and then moving out to other places around town. I did all the administrative work at home, and had set up a small office there. Reich was worried at that time that I would leave. He even feared that I would become an enemy and slander him. Therefore he used exactly the same stratagems to protect himself that he had furiously attacked in others, especially in the Stalinists. He demanded again and again that I write "confessions" about my feelings of fear of the work, occasional feelings of fear and hate about him, and he took these "confessions" and locked them away. I guess that they are still somewhere in the archives. I had to give him once a statement about all the things he had given me during the years of our marriage, including such items as birthday and Christmas gifts, and payments of hospital bills during my confinement and operation. He offered me at that time the house in Forest Hills, and was willing to have it put in my name.

But I refused it. All my life I have had the conviction that I can stand on my own feet and earn a living no matter where. Anyway, I felt that Reich needed the money from the sale of the house for his research work. Again, I had to give him a long formal statement about this. Friends and family often scolded me for my action. They said that for myself this attitude was all right, but I should have thought about the child. Although Reich did make provisions for the child later on, they were not adequate, and it is true that it was often not easy to make ends meet. Peter had to work summers from the age of fourteen to help with his educational expenses, and I had to work very hard at times to combine my own studies for a degree in education with earning a living. I think that in the long run it was a good experience for both Peter and me, and I have never regretted the refusal of the house.

I was tempted during that winter of 1952–1953 on several occasions to leave Reich and the work, but I felt that the child still needed both parents, and I did not want to separate Reich from his son who was such a comfort and joy to him. So I stayed on. I took one step, though, that Reich very much appreciated. At a meeting of the officers of the Wilhelm Reich Foundation sometime early in 1953, I resigned from the board. I continued my work as administrative director, but I felt that I could no longer function in any decision-making concerning the research work because I simply did not understand what was going on. And I have not forgotten that after that meeting one of the physicians, a member of the board, came to me and said, "I wish I had your courage."

There were several organized attacks in the beginning of 1953 against orgonomy; the medical orgonomists in particular were attacked by the American Medical Association and the American Psychiatric Association. It was obvious that these groups were still busy with their concerted efforts to destroy Reich and his work. Several of the orgonomists had received letters of warning about their association with Reich, and attacks in lectures were again reported. But still we thought that these attacks would eventually die out.

Early in 1953 I had decided that I had to discuss my situation with someone who knew Reich's work but was outside his sphere of influence, and I made plans to go to England for a few weeks to see my family. My brother had become a psychiatrist and was very familiar with Reich's writings. I had tried on several occasions to clarify my doubts about some of Reich's assertions, which were only indirectly connected with his scientific research, by talking to one or the other of the orgone therapists around him, but each time I had hit against a wall of either disapproval or blind discipleship. There was an absolute belief in everything Reich said, whether it was against all logical appearances or not.

From the beginning of his CORE program, and especially during the Oranur Experiment, Reich had kept the American government informed about what he was doing. After he had written to them about the very high counts obtained with Geiger counters at Orgonon, there were several occasions when airplanes from a nearby air force base flew very low over Orgonon, definitely circling the region. My guess was that they were checking these reports, taking counts of their own, and that they may have been worried about a nuclear plant being built there. But Reich's interpretation was totally different. He was convinced—and held on to this conviction until his death in prison—that responsible officials of the air force and the president of the United States were aware of the importance of his work but were not at liberty to come out openly for him. He asserted often that he had unknown, powerful friends who were protecting him from his enemies. For years to come Reich held on to that story, that the air force and the president were protecting him, and he would point to planes and jets flying frequently over the Rangeley region, probably on routine flights, saying that they were watching and protecting him.

One of the theories that Reich developed during those years was that the spacemen knew how to use orgone energy, that their machines, their spaceships, were running on orgone energy, and that what Reich called DOR was the offal, the exhaust of their machines.

Maybe in times to come Reich's theory will be proven correct. I still do not understand it, and I am not able to accept it on belief. But many around Reich did, and one was not allowed to question their belief.

Reich encouraged my plan for a vacation in England, and I left at the end of May 1953. Peter was to spend most of that period with Eva and her husband. Reich considered our temporary separation as a time for a clean-up, and the letters he wrote to me in England were great attempts at straightening out our relationship.

One letter written at that time shows the tenor of all that I received during my stay in England.

June 4, 1953, 1 pm

My dear:

This morning, when I had your two letters, I found myself writing a love letter to you. There was *some* hesitation in me because of the things that happened to me several times when I tried to be close to you. The "runner," you know. But this time I feel somewhat safer, although I still do not quite grasp the change. I had similar feelings when, after 16 years of agony, Eva turned around and stopped running away from me.

I must confess being in a terrific upheaval myself. Things are changing crucially within and without me. And I am glad to be able to write to you about it. Being much alone with myself, seeing no one, matters of uncertainty sometimes reach high peaks of despair. . . .

He went on to say that he did not wish to bother me with his troubles, and that I should get a good rest. He ended by saying,

I miss you very much and am afraid something might happen that could destroy the blossoming flower of a new way of being together. . . .

In another letter he mentioned his doubts whether I would return; he said that he had asked Peter, who had come back to Orgonon by the middle of June, whether he thought that I would return. Reich wrote that Peter paid me a great compliment by saying "of course she'll come back, she loves us." I had planned to take a boat back at the beginning of July, but Reich kept begging me for an earlier return by plane. I took a plane back on June 30, and was met half-way between Quebec and Rangeley by Reich and Peter, who gave me a beautiful Indian silver bracelet as a "welcome home" present.

During my absence, Reich had had an addition built to the lower cabin which would serve as his study, and the entire cabin had been prepared for winter living so that we would be able to spend the coming winter there, all three of us together. We were all looking forward to a more settled and peaceful life.

In the spring of 1953, *The Murder of Christ* had been published by Orgone Institute Press in a limited, numbered edition, not available on the open market. The thesis of *The Murder of Christ* is briefly this: Christ represents Life per se. Armored man cannot tolerate any manifestation of life or aliveness and therefore has to kill it wherever he finds it. Thus, the murder of Christ is re-enacted over and over again in all spheres of human life—in family life, in politics, in education, in science, in the name of organized religion, and in the name of charity and love. Reich tries to define the original meaning of sin, and he sees a universal sickness in the emotional plague reactions of armored mankind. It is an intensely personal book, and as Neill put it, Reich tried to get rid of his hate in *Listen, Little Man,* and now he tried to conquer his hate and his love in *The Murder of Christ*. The book made quite an impact on many of Reich's friends and students, and I remember that he received a great many comments on it. The only one that I have on hand, however, is a very long letter that Neill wrote to Reich at that time, and some quotations from the letter will show the impact of the book better than I could ever describe it:

The Murder of Christ is easily the most important book I have ever read. . . . I grasp it with my head, my eyes, my ears, but not with my guts. It shows me so clearly the gulf between the man of talent (me) and the man of universal insight (you). Do you recall our discussing the idea of my coming out to run a school in Orgonon? Your idea in 1948. I knew it could not be, knew that the danger would be that I become your disciple. Your Garden of Gethsemane, Oranur, was simply a Wiederholung [repetition] of the evils of discipleship. It troubles me. The seer, whether a Jesus a Ghandi a Reich cannot contact even his nearest ones; he must stand alone in essence. . . . You got rid of your hate in the Little Man and your love in the Christ book, not got rid of, but conquered your hate and your love. . . . Your book has stirred me up so much. It also troubled me. It is also the story of your tragedy, of a prophet who in essence feels as lonely as Jesus must have felt. You grew away from us all. Jesus was tempted to become a Führer, to save mankind. You were tempted to save mankind from atomic disaster. You both went off the rails. Poor old Jesus was not permitted to try again, but you are luckier, for you have tried again and tried in a better way than Oranur. This Christ book is of much more value than all your Oranur experiments, your equations, your

Bions. You may reply that you came to Christ via Bions, etc. True, my point is that if all your other works were lost this new book would contain them all in a way that the reading man would understand with his guts. . . .

Do you recall my little joke in the 1948 Conference when I said that one day people would be bottling holy Orgone water if you didn't look out. Your book suggests to me that that danger may not be far off. Because you refuse to be a Führer you are alone in Rangeley; because you refuse to raise their Lazaruses and make the halt and blind sound, your multitudes will seek to touch the hem of your garment—modern version—sitting in the Box. . . . Recognition. How you hate that word. "Let them come to me: I won't go to them." You and I have fought about this since 1938. You always seem to take it that I want you to be recognised by the Einsteins, Bernals, Haldanes, wanting them to assure me that you really are right. But I think of recognition in another way; I think of reaching as many as possible. I'd publish your Christ at 20 cents and broadcast its message to the world. After all the Bible is still a best seller in the world market. . . . Why should you hide your light under a bushel? What will happen to you is that after your death your disciples will write their Gospels and some hateful St. Paul will dub you Saint Willy and transport you to the clouds and pilgrims will come from Farmington to be "saved" by sitting in Oranur rays. And a Judas will get his 30 pieces of silver by writing you up in the screaming press. I say that the only way to preserve your message in its original form is to broadcast it to the four winds. . . .

At the end of July and during August, Dr. Raknes and Dr. Hoppe came to Orgonon to learn directly about the Oranur experiment and the cloudbuster. Dr. Hoppe was especially interested in the rainmaking aspects of the cloudbuster and, as far as I know, had tried again and again to get the Israeli government interested in that part of Orgonomy.

Eva Reich and her husband, the painter William Moise, had come to Rangeley to assist with the cloudbusting experiments. In 1952 they had settled in Hancock, Maine, a location on the coast where they could combine their professions. They had met some of the commercial blueberry growers, who suffered severely that summer of 1953 from a prolonged drought situation. Reich offered to draw rain for the growers within a period of twelve hours, and started the experiment in Hancock on Monday, July 6, 1953, at 10:30 A.M. The weather bureau prediction for that period was thirty-six hours of continued dry weather. At 10 P.M. that same day, rain began to fall, and there was an accumulation of 1.74 inches during the next three days. This was a very encouraging result, Reich felt, and he began to make plans for a desert expedition.

When Reich had written to Neill about his work and successes with rainmaking, Neill was worried that Reich might end up being known as "the rainmaker," to which Reich answered in August 1953, "I won't go down in history as the rainmaker, since I'm careful in maintaining my already famous status as the discoverer of cosmic Orgone Energy, the Life Energy. It is really the Oranur Experiment which puts the foundation under my whole scientific and personal existence."

In the fall of 1953 Reich read several books about flying saucers. He immediately connected the many phenomena he had observed in the atmosphere with spaceships, and from then on he tried to put all the spaceship reports and phenomena on an orgonomic basis. He was convinced of the existence of spaceships—as were very many others all over the world—and became more and more involved in this problem. It became very personal to him. He believed that spaceships were landing near Orgonon, that he was able to make contact with them by means of the cloudbuster which became a spacegun. Although he did not want to ascribe to them harmful intentions, he still blamed them for some happenings at Orgonon for which he did not seem able to find a logical explanation. For instance, Reich had been given a beautiful German shepherd dog in March 1953; a year or so later the dog was found one day with a badly broken hindleg—which may have been caused by an encounter with a car. Reich was never willing to accept a more-or-less reasonable explanation for this happening. He shrouded it in mysterious hints, indicating that he suspected either malicious humans or spacemen of venting their hatred of Reich's work on his dog.

In the following years he would state on several occasions that he was convinced the earth was under attack from outer space, and that in his work with cosmic orgone energy he held one of the keys to successfully dealing with this menace. When he later referred to his top-secret work, my guess is that he meant this particular theory. He felt he was working in the national interest of the United States.

Despite his best of intentions, the expected peacefulness of the winter of 1953–1954 at Orgonon did not materialize. There were many reasons for this. For instance, quite a few of the assistants and co-workers had left and we were rather isolated. Reich felt the isolation more acutely than I; I could always find some contact with the outside world—even if it were only the PTA meetings at the Rangeley school—while Reich was not willing or able to communicate outside his sphere.

One of the outlets he found at that time was drink. Until then, he had always enjoyed drinking on a moderate scale, and no one, until that time, had ever seen him in the slightest affected by drink. But now it was as if he had to get away from everybody and everything into complete oblivion, and he often drank himself into an absolute stupor. At other times, drink would make him furiously angry, and at such times it was safer to be out of his way. The amazing thing about this was that after a good sleep he would never show any signs of aftereffect, except that he would be absolutely furious if either Peter or I so much as hinted at his condition of the night before. Few people knew of this process in Reich; he himself tried to keep it from the knowledge of all but those intimately connected with him.

When the Food and Drug Administration attack began in earnest in February 1954 with the injunction against distribution of orgone energy accumulators, Reich directed his whole fury against the outside world at me.

It may seem that I abandoned Reich at the time of his greatest need for comfort, when the many attacks against his work had culminated in active interference by a government agency. But those who were close knew, and I have tried to explain in the previous pages, that the separation had been long in coming. I hope I made it clear that it was really a question of life or death for me at that time, that if I wanted to save any kind of self-respect and integrity I could not go on living with a man who kept shouting at me at the slightest provocation that I was a murderer, that I belonged with all those who murder life wherever it tries to function in a healthy way. I understood rationally that he was not talking to me, Ilse, his wife, that he did not accuse me personally of being a murderer. I understood that I only represented the outside world that he detested so and that was attacking him. Still, I just could not bear any longer to be made the butt of his wrath. My final, personal separation from Reich came in June 1954, but in order to bring my own work completely up to date I stayed at Orgonon until the middle of August of that year.

The period that followed was for Reich one of continuous work to defeat the FDA injunction and develop the cloudbuster—specifically, to attempt to bring rain to the desert regions.

Reich's main argument against the legal procedures throughout the whole trial period was that no court of law could judge his scientific discovery. He would be willing to cooperate with and explain his discoveries to open-minded scientists who would come without preconceived ideas, willing to see and to learn, but he would not cooperate with people whom he considered under orders from red fascism, out to destroy his good name and good work for their evil purposes. He considered many government agencies, among them the Food and Drug Administration, as communist infiltrated. He would not and could not compromise; if the law were wrong, then the law had to be changed, even if it meant that he must go to jail. Any cooperation with the court on the injunction would in essence be granting the court the right to judge scientific work, and this was out of the question for Reich. He also refused to argue his case on the level of their accusations.

The injunction itself really was an insult not only to the ideals of fair play and fairness, but even to simple legal standards. Case histories were taken from many Orgone Institute Press publications and cited out of context; mentions were made of only the positive results, although in many of these cases, in the orginal publications, it was again and again stated that there were "no cures" and that often the positive results obtained at first were followed by further deterioration and/or death. These fractional case histories were the "proof" offered by the FDA that there was a "promotion of cures." They brought into the injunction regarding interstate shipment of orgone energy accumulators each and every discovery of Reich, even those that were of a purely physical nature and had nothing whatever to do with his work with human beings. And, worst of all, they included in the injunction the sale of *all* literature published by Orgone Institute Press, including books that Reich had written long before the discovery of orgone energy, and others that had absolutely nothing to do with accumulators, such as *Mass Psychology of Fascism*; *Character Analysis*; *Listen, Little Man*; *The Murder of Christ*; *People in Trouble*; *Ether, God and Devil*; *Cosmic Superimposition*. These were included simply because some of them contained such words as "cancer" or "blood," even though these words were used in an altogether different context. The FDA considered all these books "labeling" or "promotional material" and therefore their sale was included in the injunction.

The prosecuting district attorney in the case was the same man who only a few years before had been Reich's lawyer. He was the legal adviser of the Wilhelm Reich Foundation until 1952, had drawn up the incorporation papers for the foundation, and he had attended board meetings of the foundation in 1952 where the actions of the Food and Drug Administration were discussed.

After the receipt of the injunction, Reich wrote a response to the presiding judge in Portland in which he explained in detail his refusal to cooperate. But Judge Clifford nevertheless signed the decree of injunction in March 1954, and thus the process of law had to run its course. There was an Order to Show Cause for May 5, at which time our lawyer filed an intervention; an opposition to this intervention was filed by the District Attorney on May 12. There were appeals filed during 1954 and 1955; there were hearings in July, October, and November, 1955. This legal procedure went on, back and forth, until it ended with the trial in the Federal Courthouse in Portland, Maine, on May 3, 4, 5 and 7, 1956. But more about this later.

At first the entire legal process was for Reich not much more than a great nuisance. He felt at times that although the injunction might succeed in destroying a small part of his work, it might in a way free him from some time-consuming administrative work, thus leaving him free to concentrate on his main task in cosmic engineering, desert work, and cloudbusting.

In August of 1954 he wrote in one of his letters to Neill that he was far out in space, as it were, and he mentioned his great interest in outer space. Reich was a strong supporter of Eisenhower, and he was convinced that he would receive strong support from government quarters in his drought combat. His optimism regarding the injunction was expressed in these words: "We have won the case *factually.*" But he also added that although the FDA case was dead and their assault smashed to bits, another might still succeed. In another letter he wrote: "I am not going under yet. One does not do such big things as I do without the risk of breaking one's neck, and should I ever break my neck, it would make quite a bit of noise."

He was in a fighting mood, and saw in each and every criticism the hand of red fascism. People who wrote unfavorable reviews, the agents of the FDA, well-meaning people who misunderstood this or that aspect of his work—all became tools of the red fascists and part of their conspiracy against orgonomy.

But all this interference and Reich's preoccupation with his fight against the emotional plague did not in the least diminish his activities with his real work or with his plans for a scientific expedition to the desert regions of the southwest. The encouraging results of his rainmaking operations on the east coast made it imperative for him to try them on a larger scale. He was very optimistic about the outcome of the expedition and about his final victory over his enemies. He was convinced that his truth would win out over the plague attacks.

A great shock for Reich that summer was the loss of one of his closest co-workers. Dr. Wolfe died on July 29, 1954. Although he had been ill and away from his close collaboration with Reich for over two years, his death was a great shock to all of us. He had been, all during the forties, such an integral part of Reich's work that the loss was a heavy one.

I left Orgonon in August 1954 not knowing what I should do, where I would find a job and a place to live. I had $400 in my pocket, and left most of my belongings for the time being at Orgonon. Peter went to live with Eva and Bill Moise in Hancock, Maine. It was understood that all of them, along with one of Reich's assistants who was most interested in the cloudbuster activities—Robert McCullough and his family—would move with Reich to Arizona for OROP DESERT (Orgone Energy Operation in the desert). Peter drove out with his brother-in-law, while Eva accompanied her father in his car. The trip to Arizona is one of the highlights of Peter's childhood memories, and for years afterwards he would talk about this unforgettable ride.

In October, 1954, they settled on a fairly large property outside of Tucson. Peter was enrolled in a local public school, and the work with the cloudbusters began. All activities of the foundation were transferred to the location in Tucson, which was named Little Orgonon. From reports in newspapers it seems that there was a very definite success, that rain was produced, and that previously dried-out sections showed new life. So great was public interest that the entire procedure was televised in Arizona, and Reich planned to investigate further possibilities in California.

The expedition in Tucson was joined in November by Grethe Hoff a young divorced woman, and her small child; Grethe was a former student of Reich's. Although Peter had known Grethe most of his life and was very fond of her, he found it difficult to be no longer the only child in a sort of family setup, and to have to take on the role of an older brother. But I think it was good for him to get an idea of what it means not to be an only child. However, when the expedition was completed in April 1955, having accomplished what Reich had come to do, Peter preferred to join me rather than to return either to Hancock or to Orgonon, especially since everybody's plans for the immediate future seemed to be rather vague.

Peter at age eleven came to live with me in April and stayed with me from then on, except for short vacations with his father. I was working at that time as housemother, bookkeeper, secretary, and tutor at the Hamilton School in Sheffield, Massachusetts and had begun my studies for a degree in education. It was a good atmosphere for Peter.

Reich returned to Orgonon to write up the experiences gained during OROP DESERT, and also to collect material to prove the conspiracy against his work as he saw it—as an attack by the emotional plague not just on him, but on all decent work, and on good government and rational justice.

In Oslo, I talked at length to Grethe, the woman who shared Reich's life during this period. Many of the agonies that I had experienced during my last years with Reich were repeated in her experiences. Accusations of infidelity during the last month of their life together when the relationship had deteriorated—interestingly enough with some of the same men that had figured in his accusations of me—demands of confessions, often heavy drinking, and frightening moments such as the time when Reich was shooting with his shotgun to scare off FDA agents who had come for further investigations, alternated for Reich with short periods of great insight and lucidity about his own behavior and situation. In spite of his loving attitude toward her most of the time, she was unable and unwilling to take this continuous upheaval, and left him and Orgonon at the end of June to return to her native Oslo.

I have pointed out before that Reich was absolutely convinced he had a great protector in Eisenhower and in some high officials of the air force. I do not know on what facts he based his belief, but I, for one, have never been able to accept this as a fact. He was so sure of his idea that he made an effort to equip Orgonon to receive any high official. Much of the laboratory equipment had been sold to pay for legal fees and the experimental work. The laboratory hall on the first floor of the Observatory was now emptied of all equipment. Beautiful new rugs and furnishings were bought and installed, a complete dining room set in one part, and comfortable chairs and settees in front of the fireplace in the other part. Reich even purchased new china, glass, and silverware, but none of this was very much used, since Reich was never again to stay in the observatory for more than brief vacations.

Reich was never able to live without the companionship of a woman for any length of time. When he now found himself completely alone, he telephoned me on July 14, 1955, and begged me to come back. I told him immediately that I could not go back to him, and to make my refusal quite clear I wrote him the following letter.

I would like to come back to our telephone talk of today, Thursday, and I think it would be good for all concerned if the issues were made quite clear and straight. I would not, ever, consider coming to Rangeley or Orgonon to live there. It took me more than a year now to get myself untangled from the total situation there and I most certainly do not want to get involved in any way with what is happening there.

I told you the other day that I am firmly convinced of the existence of the orgone energy and of its efficiency in its accumulated form in the various accumulators. I know that your psychiatric theories and insights, in so far as I can follow them, are sound and a great gift to the world, just as the orgone accumulators are, but I cannot and could not follow anything beyond that and I do not want to do so now. Therefore, besides the actual fact that I am employed by the Hamiltons and have some very definite assignments for August, I would not under any circumstances come to Rangeley or Orgonon.

Now to Peter: When he came back from Orgonon in June, he told me that he does not want to go back for the time being. He wants very much to be loyal to you, and he feels in a way bad that he does not want to be there now. I think, too, it makes him very unhappy every time you call and ask him to come to have to find an excuse because he is afraid of hurting you if he tells you that he does not wish to come at this time.

Besides that, I, too, feel that now is not the right time for him to come. When he came back, he told me that there are a few things that he cannot discuss with me because you do not want him to do so, and these things, I guess, puzzle him. You told me yourself on Wednesday that the situation there is so frightening that Grethe left and even Tom is very much afraid. Under these circumstances, I do not think that it is the right situation to put Peter in at this point. . . .

I hope you will feel that this letter is written in the spirit of friendship and in order to preserve a happy relationship between you and Peter. . . .

Gladys Wolfe, Dr. Wolfe's widow, who over the years had been in contact with Reich and his work and who has been a very good and helpful friend to Peter and me, remembers well the tragic loneliness of Reich during that summer, as do some other former students. One of them recalls that she met Reich in the village one evening and to her great astonishment he invited her to the movies. Another time, when she saw him in a restaurant, he invited her for a drink. And Gladys Wolfe remembers how when she met Reich in a store, he invited her for a drive to the Height of the Land—a beautiful scenic view of the Rangeley Region. But on the way, during a conversation, Reich suddenly became so furious that he turned around, deposited her at her car, and drove away. An hour later he came down to her cabin, apologized for his behavior, and stayed for a drink—but she recalls this as a rather frightening episode. Another time, when Gladys learned that he lived mostly on potatoes from the garden, which he boiled for himself, she told him of a picnic ham she had all prepared at home and Reich asked her to bring it to Orgonon. She told me that she will never forget the pathetic efforts Reich made to be the perfect host at dinner in that rather formal dining room. He had dressed up, while she arrived with her picnic basket for what she thought would be a very informal sort of dinner. The entire episode had something unreal about it, like a play. After dinner Reich played the organ and later in a conversation mentioned that he was rereading Rousseau and also the New Testament. She remembers sensing in Reich a need to be reassured that he was able to communicate, that he was not mad, that he was understood.

With the loneliness and frustration of that summer, his basic optimism must have faltered. Reich must often have sensed that the final outcome might be rather grim. His health was not good; his heart was bothering him, and his heavy drinking did not help the situation. He had always been concerned about what would happen to his remains if he should die, and he now began to prepare in earnest for a tomb—or a mausoleum—at Orgonon. I mentioned earlier the one spot on the hill where the observatory was built, where often before he had said he would like to be buried. He now had Tom Ross, the caretaker, begin digging out a place for a tomb.

He also wrote, on September 8, to Jo Jenks, the sculptress, who had earlier that year made two small reproductions of the "Rock Woman" for Reich—one in clay and one in bronze; he requested either the large original of that sculpture, or the original of another one of her statues, a standing woman, slightly bent over, for his grave. A fragment of that letter is reproduced in this book because it shows his little sketch of the sculpture and is also a good sample of his handwriting.

There was a conference of the orgonomists at Orgonon late in August 1955 where Reich gave a report on OROP DESERT, and discussed the legal situation. His frame of mind and his evaluation of the deeper meaning of the attack on him show in a letter to Neill of August 29, 1955, in which he writes: ". . . Don't you see, old Neill, that your whole world of liberal respect for neurotics is breaking down—that you must not confuse the *reality* of pathological man with the *principle* of the *dignity* of man of Locke. The whole human world was brought to the abyss by such liberal confusion. . . ."

The legal situation had now reached the point where a charge of criminal contempt of court had been brought against Reich, The Wilhelm Reich Foundation, and Dr. Michael Silvert—a New

York orgonomist who had taken it upon himself to continue the distribution of the orgone enery accumulators to patients he, as a physician, felt would profit. Reich spent most of that fall working out his plans to defeat his opponents by putting the entire procedure on a different plane. He felt that the case of the injunction should be judged not by a court of law, but by a "Board on Social Pathology." There were two court hearings, one in October and one in November, where Reich asked the court for the establishment of such a Board. The judge told him that such was not in the power of the court. Reich also asked at that hearing to be granted the right not only to represent himself and the Wilhelm Reich Foundation, but also to be recognized as representing the "Emotional Plague Prevention Office." The request was not granted. In this hearing he also stated on several occasions that he felt he was not at liberty to disclose certain facts in his defense, because to mention them in public might be against national interests.

I think one has to recognize, as painful as the admission may be, that Reich's logic had carried him on and on, so far out into space that at some point he began sometimes to lose contact with reality. He was able to pull himself back again and again, but the continued pressure forced him to seek escape into the outer regions, into a more benevolent world.

Reich never had had much of a sense of humor, he always had taken himself and his work dead-seriously without being able from time to time to poke fun at himself. Now this deadly seriousness came ever more to the foreground. He continuously coined new terms to designate the character of his attackers: HIG—Hoodlum in Government; MODJU—a synonym for emotional plague character which Reich derived by combining the names of two people who stood as symbols for the emotional plague, Mocenigo and Djugashvilli (Stalin) ; Emotional Plague Prevention Office; and so on. He expected everybody to accept these terms in their deepest, most serious meaning. He also began to speak of himself as the Discoverer, and his identification with Christ became stronger. To my mind—and I want to stress again that I am not judging Reich or analyzing him, but wish simply to state the situation as I saw it—there was a great deal of rationality in much of Reich's defensive and offensive approach to the legal procedure and in his activities in general. But there were also some definite points where I feel he went off : his belief that he was doing top secret work under the personal protection of the air force and the president of the United States ; his theory that the earth was being attacked from outer space and that only with the help of orgonomy could mankind be saved from this menace ; his belief in a communist-inspired, Moscow-directed, personal conspiracy against himself and his work.

A number of Reich's former friends and co-workers were then and still are convinced that even those points I just mentioned were completely rational and supported by facts, and I have no quarrel with them. But for myself—I can only say how I saw it then, and still see it today.

During the conference at the end of the summer of 1955, Reich met a young biologist who had for years been one of his admirers. She was eager to share his life. Aurora Karrer lived and worked in Washington, D.C., and I think she was one of many reasons that Reich decided to move to Washington for the winter. Among other reasons was Reich's desire to be closer to the seat of government. He lived there in a small hotel suite under an assumed name, Walter Roner, to keep unwanted intruders out. I do not know too much about Reich's relationship with Miss Karrer. She was an attractive young woman, considerably younger than Reich, in fact the same age as his daughter Eva, and very devoted to him. At times life with Reich must have been too much for her too, because she would sometimes disappear for days on end without warning Reich. I have been told by several people, including Miss Karrer herself after Reich's death, that Reich had intended to marry her soon after his release from prison.

Eva Reich and her husband also followed Reich to Washington. Reich liked Washington, and thought of it as a very functional city. Peter visited his father there during his Christmas and February vacations, and enjoyed exploring the city and its surroundings with him. Reich spoke of acquiring a small estate in Maryland or Virginia, but it never materialized.

My relationship with Reich after our separation was good. We had a great deal of correspondence, and continued to share important decisions regarding Peter. I think that Reich was impressed by my efforts to establish a new life and profession, and I was told by many friends that he always spoke very positively about me. It was one of the strange contradictions about the man that during these last two years he sent me expensive birthday and Christmas presents, often quite a bit more extravagant than those he had given me before. And although his $75-a-month allowance for Peter was rather small compared to his own style of life, he did occasionally buy very good clothes for his son, and was willing to contribute more for his education.

However, there were also during that period occasional upsetting, bitter telephone calls from Reich whenever he felt that anyone was trying to influence Peter against him, or that I might not agree with some arrangements he had made for or during Peter's visits to him. Although I had been officially appointed as Peter's legal guardian at the time of our separation, I preferred to have Reich's approval on decisions regarding our son, and when I made plans for taking Peter with me for a vacation to England during the summer of 1956 I asked Reich not to put any obstacles in my way. The boy would not have enjoyed the trip if he had felt that his father disapproved of it.

Reich gave his blessing to the trip but he did not really want Peter to go, and the child felt it. In March 1956 Reich wrote to Neill, "Peter told me he does not want really to go to England this summer. He expressed fear to get stuck there and not be able to return to the U.S.A. He wants to become a flier, a pilot. He is my best, 'little' friend. He visited me twice here in Washington. He partook fully, consciously and enthusiastically in our Desert work in Arizona. He knows much already about natural science and about DOR emergency."

But in the end Peter did go with me to England, and that visit came very close to ending the long friendship between Reich and Neill.

Before that summer, however, came the terrible ordeal of the jury trial in Portland, Maine on May 3, 4, 5, and 7, 1956.

The Trial
of May 3, 4, 5, and 7, 1956

I have tried in previous pages to show something of the background that led to the trial. From the time he received the injunction in February 1954, until the final disposition in 1957, Reich spent a large part of his time away from his scientific investigations, working on the issues involved in the legal attack on his work. He saw this attack not only as a personal one, but as an example of broader human problems; for him it involved the basic injustice of sterile, dead laws directing vital, individual thinking. He was upset not so much by his own case as by what he felt to be the universal problems of human decency, of what is good and alive in man, having to fight for survival against intolerance, bigotry, and plain indecency.

131

I think I understand the thoughts that lay behind his approach, because I knew his way of thinking for a long time. But Reich's attempt to fight the purely legalistic process of the injunction with universal concepts of law led to an impasse. He expressed often the idea that if the laws were wrong, then he, Reich would change the laws. Reich's writings were never easy to read, and his letters to the judge, his explanations at the hearings, his talks to the jury were to a large extent incomprehensible. It was as if this case were fought on several levels which rarely met. The government fought its case against Wilhelm Reich; Wilhelm Reich fought his case against not only a government agency, but against a communist conspiracy he saw behind the government. Reich fought his case against evil in general.

Reich had always felt a certain distrust of lawyers. He now refused legal help, except occasionally in a counselling capacity. As I have mentioned earlier, there were so many misrepresentations, misinterpretations, and outright lies contained in the original injunction that it should have been easy on this basis alone to have it squelched. But Reich refused again and again to fight this case on "their" level. Their approach represented what he had much earlier termed the Emotional Plague that he hoped to smash once and for all.

I think it would be rather difficult for an outsider to disentangle the various threads that in Reich's thinking all came together in one red thread of a communist-inspired and -directed conspiracy, beginning with the Einstein Affair in 1941 and ending in the Food and Drug Administration attack in court in 1954. There does not seem to be any doubt that concerted efforts were made against Reich and his work by such organizations as the American Medical Association and the American Psychiatric Association. Such attacks were again and again reported to Reich by his medical colleagues and co-workers; they also appeared in the professional periodicals, as in the *Journal of the AMA* (January 1949), or the *Bulletin of the Menninger Clinic* (March 1948). Reich would attribute these attacks to the deeply imbedded fear human beings have of recognizing the core of moving sensations in the human body. This was the sphere of the orgone therapist, as opposed to what he felt to be the static psychological and neurological concepts of traditional medicine and psychiatry. He also ascribed the attacks to professional jealousy because the orgone therapists were much sought after and enjoyed great esteem because of their successful therapeutic approach.

In a letter to Neill of June 14, 1955, Reich includes the "rich U.S. manufacturers of drugs" in the conspiracy, adding that "there is lots of information to the effect that [they] were in collusion with and incited by Russian Red Fascists. These, i.e., Stalin, were the teachers in method of both the Hitlers and the McCarthys. Once the whole thing will be over, you will know the whole truth. . . ."

There appeared during the court action the almost incredible evidence of an investigation by the Food and Drug Administration, carried on for a period of seven years with often very malicious and defamatory overtones; it was definitely not a scientific and unbiased investigation. FDA agents interviewed hundreds of people —laymen and physicians—but they were unable to uncover any false claims, any harmful effects, or any "sex cult" in Reich's work. Many people were willing to give statements about the beneficial use of the accumulator, none of which was brought in as evidence. The FDA had to resort to planted receivers of orgone energy accumulators in order to find witnesses against the foundation, and the evidence of the FDA's alleged control experiments has never been introduced in court.

But real as these attacks were in their intensity and in their painful effect on Reich, it is difficult to believe that they were part of a communist-inspired and -directed attack aimed at stealing the beneficial results of orgonomy for Russia while at the same time destroying this work in the United States to the detriment of the national interest.

At the various court hearings Reich hinted again and again that national security prevented his revealing some pertinent facts. He believed himself to be engaged in top secret work of such a delicate nature that even though his life and the continuation of his work might be in danger, the government was not in a position to come to his rescue. I am convinced that somewhere in his reasoning he counted on a last minute, sensational rescue through intervention by his "powerful allies," maybe even the president himself.

During all this time the serious press was either silent or it joined in the attack. Again and again, the original smear that had appeared early in 1947 in the *New Republic* served as sole basis for a continuing number of articles, not only in the more lurid popular magazines—who added their own pornographic interpretations— but also in such periodicals as *The Saturday Review of Literature* (August 1947, January 1953), the *McGill Daily* (Montreal, December 1947), *Colliers* (December 1947), *The Sunday Compass* (August 1950) to name just a few. After the injunction was served in February 1954, a number of the Maine daily newspapers published articles about it, some favorably recalling Reich's successful rain-making experiments in the Hancock, Maine region.

It may clarify the sequence of events if I recapitulate briefly the course of the legal procedures. The Injunction, restraining the Wilhelm Reich Foundation, Wilhelm Reich, and Ilse Ollendorff from shipping orgone energy accumulators and the literature of Orgone Institute Press through interstate commerce was filed and served on us on February 10, 1954. My name was later removed as, after August 1954, I was no longer an employee of either the foundation or Reich.

Reich, in an answer to the injunction, wrote a lengthy Response to Judge Clifford in Portland, Maine on February 25, in which he denied the government's right to judge (and interfere in) natural scientific work dealing with basic natural law. This response did not comply with acceptable legal procedures, and was not regarded by the court as a legal answer to the injunction. Therefore, a Decree of Injunction was obtained by the FDA by default in March 1954. This decree ordered the destruction of all accumulator devices, the withholding from distribution of all of Reich's previously published hardcover books, and the destruction of all journals, annals, bulletins, pamphlets and other publications of Orgone Institute Press. They were all regarded as "labeling" for the accumulator, irrespective of the fact that many of the books had been written long before the discovery of orgone energy and dealt with psychiatric, mass-psychological, biographical material, or with purely biophysical phenomena. An appeal was filed with the court immediately.

In October 1954 Orgone Institute Press informed the court that it would resume its distribution of literature, and that the Orgone Institute would continue its scientific work.

In January 1955 a group of medical orgone therapists asked for permission to enter the case as an interested party and also asked for a Stay of Injunction. Their intervention was refused, and the Stay of Injunction denied, with the exception of a stay of the destruction of the apparatus and the books until final determination of the appeal.

In July 1955 United States Attorney Peter Mills (again, the same man who had been the Wilhelm Reich Foundation lawyer, and who had participated in board meetings of the foundation at which the FDA investigation had been discussed) filed a criminal contempt action against the Wilhelm Reich Foundation, Wilhelm Reich, and Michael Silvert for violating the Decree of Injunction. Specifically, Reich was accused of denying information to officers of the FDA when they visited him in Tucson, Arizona in December 1954, and in Rangeley, Maine in June 1955. The Wilhelm Reich Foundation was accused of refusing to comply with the terms of the decree; Dr. Michael Silvert, a psychiatrist and medical orgonomist who had taken over some of the functions regarding the distribution of accumulators in the New York region, was accused of continuing with the distribution of accumulator devices and related printed materials. A hearing on the Order to Show Cause was to be held in regard to the criminal contempt charge in Portland, Maine on July 26, 1955. The foundation, Reich, and Silvert filed a Motion to Discharge this Order to Show Cause on July 18 through a lawyer. At the hearing of July 26 the three defendants filed a Demand for a Jury Trial.

U.S. Attorney Peter Mills filed an amendment to the information about violation of the injunction on October 11, 1955. A day later, another motion to vacate and dismiss the decree of injunction as amended was filed by Dr. Silvert's lawyer and argued in court, also in behalf of the group of orgone therapists headed by Dr. Elsworth Baker. This motion was denied by the court on October 18, in a hearing where Reich appeared in his own behalf. Reich stressed during this hearing his basic tenet that no political juridical body can judge basic natural laws and natural scientific research. He also implied at the same hearing that fraud on the part of the FDA was being perpetrated on the court through the FDA's suppression of vital evidence. Both Reich and Silvert then filed on October 24 another motion to dismiss the amended information on the ground of misrepresentation of facts. This motion was denied by the court at the next hearing which took place on November 4, 1955, in which Reich again appeared without a lawyer, representing himself.

In this hearing Reich made another motion in which he asked for dismissal of the case against orgonomy, for the establishment of a Board on Social Pathology to hear and determine this matter. The motion was denied on the ground that the court had no power to create any board. Reich then stated that he would be willing to cooperate with anyone who would take a medical and educational approach to the case—he would be completely open if the new participant were likewise open and above-board in his approach. At the same hearing Reich stated that for reasons of national security he could not disclose certain facts that might be helpful to his cause, even if his refusal to do so meant going to jail. He also hinted at a conspiracy underlying the whole prosecution.

In all of these hearings and motions Reich acted and signed as Counsel for the Defense EPPO (Emotional Plague Prevention Office) which was established for the purpose of "showing up the motives of the opponents and the fraudulence of their attack." In his November 17 motion asking for permission to inspect all materials subpoenaed by the FDA, he signed himself Counsel for the Discovery of Life Energy. This motion, too, was denied by the court.

Next was the designation of the chief judge of the U.S. District Court of Massachusetts, Acting Judge for the District of Maine, George C. Sweeney, for the criminal contempt of court trial, set finally for April 30, 1956.

The defendants as well as all witnesses had been subpoenaed to appear on April 30 in the courthouse in Portland, Maine. I was to be one of the government witnesses, and had received my subpoena in Sheffield, Massachusetts, where I was working at that time. The subpoena was signed by the clerk of the court. On April 24, I received a telegram from Reich advising me that due to the conspiratoral nature of the FDA action I should be most careful to see that all legal documents were technically correct and that it was my own responsibility to decide whether or not to obey the subpoena.

I consulted a local lawyer who told me that my subpoena was absolutely legal and had to be obeyed unless I wanted to risk a fine. Therefore, I decided to be in Portland at the designated time. However both Reich and Silvert maintained that the subpoena needed to be signed by the judge, and refused to appear. Quite a few of the witnesses, following their example, likewise refused to appear in court at that date. The two defendants had informed the court of their whereabouts, so that the U.S. marshals had no difficulty in taking them into custody in Washington, D.C. and New York respectively. The marshals brought them to Portland in handcuffs which they held up for everyone to see when they were photographed by the local press. The other witnesses then appeared on their own—and were eventually fined for disobeying the subpoena. Both Reich and Silvert were taken to jail, but released on bail on May 2, 1956.

While waiting for the trial to begin in Portland, I had been asked by both U.S. Attorney Peter Mills and the lawyer for the prosecution Mr. Joseph Maguire whether I would be willing to identify and initial some of the ledgers and other business records that I had kept as an employee of the foundation, to save time during the trial later on. I complied with their request. It was during that time that Mr. Maguire showed me a volume of collected letters and other records that Reich had reproduced by photo-offset, bound in a looseleaf binder, and given to friends of the foundation in a limited, numbered edition, with a careful check on who received it. It was entitled *Conspiracy and Emotional Chain Reaction.* I was more than surprised to see that book in Maguire's hands and took care to ascertain the number of the volume; later I learned that this particular book had been sent to Mrs. Oveta Culp Hobby, Secretary of the Department of Health, Education, and Welfare. Maguire then asked me whether I was aware of the fact that a document, signed by me, was contained in the book. I told him that I had known of it since Dr. Reich had asked my permission to put it in. I mention this, because this episode became part of the trial later on.

The trial itself began on May 3, 1956. From the very beginning Reich told the court that he did not deny having disobeyed the injunction, but he made it clear in a motion which he addressed to Judge Sweeney during the trial, that one had to distinguish between the legalistic point of view that he *did* violate the injunction, and the fact that he *had* to violate it. He asked the judge to make this distinction between *did* and *had to* clear in his instructions to the jury. This motion, like all others before it, was denied by the court. To Reich, this was the core of the problem. It came up during the examination of William Moise by Reich on May 5, when the following exchange took place between the judge and Reich.

REICH: It is a fact that I did not obey the Injunction.

THE COURT: The only question here is whether you disobeyed or did not disobey the Injunction. The Court does not recognize any excuse for not obeying it after it was issued.

REICH: May I reinforce my statement that I have disobeyed the Injunction?

THE COURT: Then what are we trying here?

REICH: That is not my question.

THE COURT: If you have admitted that you have disobeyed the Injunction, then you are really wasting our time here. I cannot listen to why you disobeyed it or why you had to. The fact is that if you admitted you disobeyed it your case is about over. I said to you, today, we are producing facts. When the case is argued by you, you have a greater range of variation to argue to the jury. You can argue, for instance, any inference that would naturally arise from the facts that have been produced. You can argue motives. You have a greater range on argument, but until you have entered a plea of guilty, we will go on with this case.

REICH: I do not plead guilty.

THE COURT: You said you disobeyed the Injunction. I do not recognize that as a valid excuse.

REICH: It is pertinent to the fact that we did not obey the Injunction.

A procession of witnesses testified to that which the defendants did not deny at all. Then small and insignificant money transactions were brought up in order to prove that the Foundation was still in business and that Reich used such monies for his private purposes. Reich pointed out on one such occasion that while the prosecution questioned the use of $21.50 for certain purposes, the books and records gave ample proof that he had invested more than $350,000 in his research over the years. Even the judge became annoyed with Maguire's questioning about these picayune matters, and during Maguire's examination of William Moise once asked pointedly: "Why don't you find out whether they paid for his cigarettes!" On another occasion the Judge showed his somewhat contemptuous attitude toward the manner in which this entire trial was conducted when in a direct questioning of U.S. Attorney Peter Mills by Reich about his previous relations to him and the Foundation, the following exchange took place.

REICH: The fact that I want to establish here is only one. You were for three years—for more than three years—a good friend of ours and a counsellor?

MILLS: That's correct. I was professionally, but not intimately.

REICH: There was some private contact?

MILLS: Yes, a cup of coffee.

THE COURT: With cream and sugar in it?

REICH: That's right!

A few minutes later, during the same examination, there was the following exchange.

REICH: My question is, under the circumstances, what reasons, or what facts induced Mr. Mills after being our counsel for three years, and I regarded him as a good friend, to be our opponent's counsel, and the one to prosecute me and Dr. Silvert as criminals?

THE COURT: That is a fair question if there is anything.

MR. MILLS: The question is, what prompted me?

DR. REICH: What made you change your mind?

MR. MILLS: I have never changed my mind. I am not conscious of changing my mind.

THE COURT: Wait a minute. The original question was, what prompted you to change sides.

MR. MILLS: I never changed sides. . . .

There was, I think also on May 5, an examination of Maguire by Reich in the course of which Reich questioned Maguire about several books and documents, among them the volume *Conspiracy and Emotional Chain Reaction.* Maguire first said that he might have seen a similar volume, and when asked specifically by Reich whether he had ever seen that book, he answered with "No." This untruth shocked me considerably, just as Mr. Mills had shocked me before that, since I remembered that on more than one occasion he had brought his wife along to Orgonon and we all had friendly, personal chats.

During a recess in the hearing I asked to see the Judge in his chambers. He was very kind and understanding when I told him of my experience with Maguire in regard to this book. He advised me to tell Reich about it, to have Reich put me on the witness stand again and to question me about this incident. I was examined about it by Reich and cross-examined by Maguire. Although Maguire made a great to-do about the fact that it would be rather easy to remove material from the binder so that one could never be sure whether it was in reality an identical volume which he had and which Reich showed him, it must have been quite obvious to the court and the jury that he was trying very hard to get out of a very uncomfortable situation by some semantic twists.

I think that Reich was very pleased with my role in the trial which made me, the government witness, one of the best witnesses in his behalf. I remember he gave me a big hug when I told him about Maguire.

During my talk with Judge Sweeney he had asked whether I thought it wise for him to request a psychiatric examination of Reich which, he felt, might possibly give Reich a way out of the proceedings. He made it quite clear to me that in the face of the repeated admission of both defendants that they had violated the injunction there was no other way to prevent their being found guilty. Judge Sweeney also said he was sorry that he had come into the picture too late to change it; too many mistakes had been made that could, at this point, not be rectified. I very vigorously advised against a psychiatric examination. First, because it would have infuriated Reich and all his friends to a great extent, and second, because whatever Reich's delusions may have been in regard to the conspiracy or to the secret nature of his work, I felt that he was absolutely rational in the conduct of the trial so far as his basic premises were concerned, namely that scientific research should be free of any kind of political interference, that he had a duty to expose the biased and malevolent intentions of the FDA investigation which he felt to be against public interest.

In the closing addresses, one again had a feeling that the two sides were speaking different languages, that the levels on which they stood and looked at the issues just did not meet. Although Reich's friends, co-workers, and followers were able to understand the reasoning of the abbreviated version of Reich's statement, Atoms for Peace versus the HIG, read by Dr. Silvert as the closing statement for the defense, neither the court nor the jury, unfamiliar with the basic premises of Reich's reasoning, understood any of it. All they could hook their rebuttal on were refutations of Reich's calling FDA agents spies and hoodlums. The prosecuting attorney, in his summation, pointed out that these FDA agents could look upon long devoted years of service for the government while, on the other hand, Reich and his followers were keeping these same agents off their premises, sometimes at gunpoint. He also brought up, as one of his rebuttals of Reich's accusation that the scientists of the FDA were not qualified to sit in judgment over orgone energy because they had not studied it, that Reich himself was not licensed as a physician in this country.

The judge then charged the jury to confine themselves strictly to the issues of the trial, which were to find whether the defendants did violate the Decree of Injunction and thus were in contempt. He described it as a simple case within the definition of the law.

Myron Sharaf, in his description of the trial in the memorial volume *Wilhelm Reich,* has presented the jury very well as looking "like a movie jury—extremely typical of the American populace, down to one Negro. There were several women—middle-aged . . . The jury was clearly the 'average citizen.' . . ." This jury then, after having listened to the judge's instructions, deliberated only about ten minutes and returned with their verdict of guilty for all three defendants—Wilhelm Reich, Michael Silvert, and The Wilhelm Reich Foundation. The Judge postponed the pronouncement of sentence until May 25, 1956.

On that day, The Wilhelm Reich Foundation was ordered to pay a fine of $10,000; Wilhelm Reich was ordered to be punished

by imprisonment for the term of two years; and Michael Silvert
was ordered to be punished by imprisonment for the term of one
year and one day.

Reich wrote, on May 25th, after receiving the sentence, the following letter to the court.

We have lost, technically only, to an incomprehensible procedure
treadmill. I and my fellow workers have, however, won our case
in the true, historical sense. We may be destroyed physically to-
morrow; we shall live in human memory as long as this planet is
afloat in the endless Cosmic Energy Ocean as the Fathers of the
cosmic, technological age. . . . I have won the battle against evil
. . . I may suffer physical disaster, but shame and dishonor are
not on my face. It is on the face of the XXth Century Judas Iscariot,
Peter Mills, who betrayed his former friends and clients when the
Oranur experiment struck us in 1952, and when the Red Fascist
Hig, under Moskau order, was out to get our experimental secrets.
. . . This important subject has been presented by me in 1953, during
the grave planetary DOR emergency, as if in anticipation of the
Hig assault. Here, the Murder of Christ 2,000 years ago has been
taken as an historical example of the method used by the Emotional
Plague of Man to kill Life and Truth. This time, however, Judas has
betrayed and the Hig is killing the scientific hope to cope with the
planetary disaster that is upon us. . . .

This statement was signed by both Reich and Silvert.

Thus ended the trial. An appeal was immediately filed with the
U.S. Court of Appeals and a request for stay of execution of sentence was granted by the court on June 4.

The Aftermath
of the Trial

Among Reich's friends and followers there was great shock and confusion. No one had really expected a prison sentence.

Reich's longstanding complaint that people came to him only to take, and never to give anything back, had proved again to be true. Of the many friends and followers only a very few, a dozen or so, had found it possible or worthwhile to be on hand in Portland to give not only some sort of moral support to Reich, but also to impress upon the court and the Jury that this was not a lone and somewhat eccentric mad scientist, but a widely known and respected psychiatrist and researcher. Too many of the orgone therapists felt they could not afford to leave their lucrative practices for a few days to stand at Reich's side, at least morally; too many of his admirers were afraid to be involved by association in work they admired but did not fully grasp. It was a small, miserable courtroom with a small, miserable number of supporters.

Upon learning of the sentence through a telephone call from Reich on May 26, I wrote him the following letter.

I think that I can express better on paper than talking over the telephone what I want to say. It was, of course, a great shock for both Peter and me, since we were prepared for a large fine, but definitely not for a prison sentence. . . .

As I told you on the phone, I realize that this whole case is on your part a matter of principle, and that you could not act differently than you did. This realization on my part, however, does not mean that I don't hate to see you become a martyr for your own cause or—in a larger sense—for humanity. I feel very strongly that you have gone your way as far as you possibly could; but that now is the time to reconsider. In order to preserve your strength for the fight on the big issues, I think you should now use the conventional legal procedures to fight the legalistic mechanisms. I do hope very much that it will be possible to reopen the whole case and that the injunction will become invalid and thus the contempt of court likewise non-existent. Maybe this is wishful thinking, and you may think me a fool or presumptuous that I even write this to you; but I know that you are not one of those people who could go easily to prison, no matter for what cause, and I don't want to see you sacrificed when there is no absolute need for it. And I still think that neither your name nor your honor would be in any way sullied by using all possible conventional legal means to fight this thing. . . .

To this letter Reich replied on May 29, from Orgonon that he appreciated and agreed with my position and might employ a good lawyer from now on.

. . . Had I gone to court originally, I would have lost my honor and would have been found *guilty* of *fraud*. I am in good spirits since I have saved the principle of the case. My personal fate may well be doubtful. But I have powerful backing. Many great people have died for far less than I am risking to die. Somehow, I feel I have won and shall win further. You are right: I would not take well to a penitentiary, and—most likely—would be killed there.

He ended the letter by thanking me for my understanding and especially for my cooperation in all things concerning Peter, and he expressed the wish to see me at Orgonon before I left for England.

I was not able to visit Reich before we left, but Peter, who was twelve years old at that time, went to Orgonon for a short visit. While there, he witnessed the destruction of the accumulators and the burning of all softcover journals, annals, bulletins, and pamphlets that had remained at the students' laboratory. Thomas Ross, the caretaker of Orgonon, recalls the destruction of the accumulators with great bitterness. The Decree of Injunction had specifically mentioned that the material of which they were made should, if possible, be salvaged. But some of the supervising FDA agents directed that the Celotex panels be slashed to such an extent that they could not be used for any kind of construction or insulation.

The same destruction was carried out in New York on August 23, 1956. The decree ordered destruction of all material pertaining directly to the use and construction of orgone energy accumulator devices. All issues of the *Orgone Energy Bulletin; Orgone Energy Emergency Bulletin; Internationale Zeitschrift für Orgonomie* (International Journal of Orgonomy) ; *Emotional Plague versus Orgone Biophysics; Annals of the Orgone Institute; Ether, God and Devil;* and *The Oranur Experiment* had to be loaded on a truck at the stockroom of Orgone Institute Press by Dr. Silvert with the help of Dr. Victor M. Sobey (a medical orgonomist) and two assistants, under the supervision of two FDA agents. At the last minute, the two FDA agents insisted that the hardcover books, i.e., *Mass Psychology, Character Analysis, Sexual Revolution, Murder of Christ, People in Trouble, Cosmic Superimposition,* and *Ether, God and Devil*—which the decree ordered only to be withheld from distribution—should also be destroyed. Dr. Sobey described this entire experience in a letter. "(We) felt like people who, when they are to be executed, are made to dig their own graves first and are then shot and thrown in. We carried box after box of the literature. No accurate check was taken of the amount, but it filled the truck. . . . After loading was completed, the truck went to the Gansevoort Incinerator at Gansevoort and Hudson Streets. It dumped its load of books into the fire, and it was done." Dr. Sobey added at the end of his report, ". . . the burning of these books is not the whole issue but is only one aspect in the murder of the truth."

With the appeal pending, and with hope still strong for the

reopening of the case and eventual vindication of Reich, there seemed to be no reason to postpone our trip to England at the end of June 1956. Before the trial, and again in June, Peter had visited his father in Washington and at Orgonon and had heard a great deal about the menace to our planet in the form of outer space flying objects. He had also become convinced that the U.S. Air Force was his father's secret ally and would protect him, Peter, in any dangerous situation anywhere in the world. In England his fears were further activated—he became convinced that he might be kidnapped—when in August I received a few telegrams and letters from Reich warning me about enemies against his work who might be out to frighten me. One telegram dated August 3 warned me to watch carefully for slander or blackmail originating from red fascists to eliminate me as a reliable witness, and a letter of the same date, punctuated by exclamation marks and underlinings, warned again that I should be most careful of what I told to whom and said that he would like to discuss things with me after my return from England.

My brother, with whom we were staying in England, also received several messages from Reich at that time, asking him to watch carefully over our safety. I did not know what Reich was referring to, and being accustomed to his often rash and impulsive reaction to any kind of rumor, I did not take this matter too seriously. But it was a rather shocking experience for both Neill and my brother, both of whom were then living not far from a U.S. Air Force base, to hear Peter say again and again when jets flew frequently overhead, "They are there to protect me, they are looking after me."

Both Neill and my brother had very positive attitudes toward Reich but were nevertheless concerned about Peter's involvement in problems that were beyond his understanding. Reich's thinking was not only likely to be misinterpreted by Peter's young mind, but perhaps was leading to a severe disturbance of the child's reality perception.

After our return to the States in September—at which time, at his expressed desire, we did not visit Reich because it did not fit in with his schedule—Neill wrote a letter to Reich telling him of his concern about Peter's involvement in his father's problems and Peter's fantasies about enemies from outer space. Reich's first reaction to this letter was a note of welcome-home to Peter in which he warned him to keep these things about outer space to himself: "You know more about it than the Neills and others." His second reaction, as I have indicated before, almost finished the long friendship with Neill.

A copy of Neill's October 1, 1956 letter to Reich with its typed-in addendum shows what happened much better than I could explain it.

My Dear Reich,
    So our long friendship has come to an end because you consider me unreliable and on the side of X. and Co. How very sad. Just at a time when you require every friend you can have too. I think you have had few friends; disciples yes, enemies yes, but few who stood as it were outside and were objective. Maybe Sigurd Hoel and I were of the few who were not yesmen. I was a friend who loved you, who recognised your genius and also the Little Man in you, but I never was a "Reichian" who accepted all you said and did. Thus I was genuinely concerned about Peter and his fears of overhead planes and his grown-up-ness which is not real, for he wants to be childish and play a lot all the time. I could speak to you of him where one of your disciples could not. I think you have suffered through too many people being afraid to challenge you in any way. I think you lost perspective, z.B. [i.e.] in seeing a danger in an ordinary Mensch like X. who has not the tact nor the knowledge to challenge your work. I think you have worried far too much about folks who were unbedeutend [insignificant].

    I wonder if you know how much you mean to many of us, and I don't mean in your work; I mean emotionally, humanly. The other day sitting with Sigurd and Raknes and Grete and Lilian Bi the warmth of their love for you, the fears for your future showed me that they cared more for Reich the man than Reich the discoverer. They are bedeutend (significant) while the Ys and Xs etc. aren't. We all felt strongly the sad fact that we were all 3000 miles from you at this anxious time of your appeal.

    Often I have heard you say: Everyone is right in some way. Now I say to you that everyone is wrong in some way also. I say that you are wrong about Peter. He looks too anxious. I think he is trying to live a part . . . "I am the only one who understands what Daddy is doing." He may understand but his emotions are all mixed up. He isn't Peter Reich; he is Peter Reich plus Wilhelm Reich.

And, dear old friend, call this emotional plague or what you will. To me it is just plain truth.

I wish you every success in your appeal against an unjust sentence. I wish you many years to continue your work.

Goodbye, Reich, and bless you,

Neill

(Addendum written by Neill on his own copy of the above letter.)

Above was written in Oslo. Grethe, Raknes and a few others, worried about Reich's legal battle, sent him a joint telegram of love and encouragement. Reich wired to Grethe: "Don't trust Neill. He is no longer to be trusted."

That followed on Ilse and Peter's visit to Summerhill when Peter talked of the USA planes overhead being sent to protect him against red fascism. I fear I laughed and he reported me to Reich as a non-believer. Peter was scared of being kidnapped then; Reich had warned him to be careful. Eine elende Geschichte. [A miserable story.] Neill.

However, it was not, as Neill had feared, the end of their friendship or their correspondence. On October 15, Reich answered Neill's letter with: "Can you be patient for a while until I am free to talk to you? Do not worry . . . ," to which brief note Neill reacted with a wonderfully understanding letter, dated October 22.

Your short letter made me cry. It seemed to symbolise your loneliness, your misery in this abominable martyrdom, yet it conveyed your courage, your belief in your faith and work. Damn this 3000 miles separation. I know only a bit of your reality over there, and can have no perspective. Yet IF you didn't attend the second summons because someone said the summons wasn't properly signed, then I am sure you got wrong advice. Such a point cannot fight a battle whereas your original trumpet call—No court has the right to judge a matter of science—was right and powerful. I make the guess that none of your workers was big enough, detached enough to give you good advice. . . .

Reich I love you. I cannot bear to think of your being punished by an insane prison sentence. You couldn't do it and you know it. I wish to God that you'd simply let some good lawyer take up your case from the legal angle. Why should anyone waste breath and time trying to explain to a judge and jury what your work is? They can't possibly understand and the reporters will make a travesty of it all in a Brady way. I think you are all wrong in thinking that the trials are instigated from Moscow. . . .

The Tatsache [fact] is that you are being crucified fundamentally because you are the first man in centuries who has preached pro-life-ness, because you were the one and only man to assert the right of adolescence to love completely. The majority in USA, Britain, Russia, in the whole world are anti-life, so that you do not need to look for specific enemies like the FDA; they are only the shot that was fired at Sarajevo, not the basic cause of the attack on you. In any court your defence should be in big letters I AM FOR LIFE AND LOVE, not I am the victim of Russia or red fascism or anything else. I confess to a feeling that you have imagined motives when the big motive of hostility was there plain to be seen. You haven't had enough normal people around you to argue the point with you. To think that the great man who has advocated ration-alism all his life would now embrace irrationalism is a terrible thought. Terrible because when you are up against the hard ration-alism of law courts you must be super-rational to win.

Sorry to lecture like this but I am concerned about you, very much so. Get that lawyer and fight them with their own legal weapons, for your weapons are invisible to them.

My love and concern and blessing.   Yours ever, Neill

On November 14, Reich the optimist writes to Neill: "The Appeal hearing went well in our favor so far. But, the enemy is tough, a killer." The same indestructible optimism and his never-resting activity show in a December 12 letter to me. ". . . I am back in top orgonometric mathematics and in painting. I miss my music. . . ."

Peter spent the Christmas vacation in Washington, where Reich had established winter quarters in a small hotel suite. He went on rides in Daddy's beautiful car. Reich had always liked good cars, and had bought for the trip to Arizona a white convertible Chrys-ler 300; for Peter this was a symbol of his father's importance. The boy was pampered by the service personnel at the hotel, and he felt himself important too. He went shopping with Reich who bought him a very beautiful winter jacket in one of the best stores in Washington. All in all, this last vacation that Peter spent with his father was a good and impressive one.

During January and February 1957 the correspondence between Reich and me, and Reich and Peter, was concerned with Peter's high school—whether to continue his public schooling or to send him to a private school. Although basically we all agreed that the public school experience was more desirable, I felt that under the circumstances a private school might be better for Peter. Another issue discussed in both letters and in telephone calls concerned dispositions Reich wanted to make in his Last Will and Testament, concerning Peter.

In a letter to Peter, dated February 20, 1957, Reich referred to the school issue and to the continued struggle in the courts. The letter was headed: PLANETARY PROFESSIONAL CITIZENS COMMITTEE—DOR EMERGENCY—Orop Ea. In it Reich expressed his hopes that he would yet succeed in getting the Supreme Court to accept his case. He mentioned his reply brief in which he had talked about the need for laws to combat powerdrunkenness, and stated, "Modju will not get away with this attempt to murder by proxy."

The last personal letter I ever received from Reich was dated March 5, 1957, a few days before he entered prison; he sent me a check for a television set as a combined birthday present for Peter and me. The letter ended: "The legal situation approaches the climax. Happy birthday—Love Wil."

Coming back to the legal situation: In October 1956 the Supreme Court had refused to hear the case and Reich's petition was denied. The brief that Reich had sent to the Court of Appeals as chief counsel for the Discovery of Cosmic Life Energy was another touching appeal to "Fairness" and to "Reason," not based on legal grounds but on truth—the actual discoveries and work in the realm of natural science. The top-secret involvement of the basic research work was also mentioned. Reich suggested as a legal basis for reversal of the court decision the fact that the *motives* of the total attack had up to that time been completely ignored. He noted that only orgone energy could help in case of interplanetary war to protect our planetary security against invaders from outer space. He noted in the brief also that the U.S. Air Force was in possession of all information regarding the use of orgone energy in possible repulsion of outer space invaders; they knew about the motor run on cosmic orgone energy, and about the entire involvement of this energy in space travel. He talked about the use of the cloudbuster as a space gun and about its more earthbound function of making the deserts green and fruitful. It is a document in which Reich tries to give a brief view of what he saw as practical applications of his discovery of the orgone energy in medicine, space travel, weather formation; also it entered upon the psychiatric, social, and philosophical—almost religious— implications of his discovery when he talked of Revelation and Delivery, coming back again and again to the planetary emergency. He restated that the injunction *had* to be violated because "the discoverer of the Cosmic Energy had during 1954–1955, the years of the injunction, fought under the very eyes of the Air Force the *First Battle of the Universe.*"

He was, of course, in the deepest sense correct when he stated that "criminal contempt . . . [had been] committed by the accuser and not by the accused," but what court of law in the world would accept these premises?

Besides this brief filed by Reich, there was a brief filed by the lawyer for the Wilhelm Reich Foundation claiming that the injunction was fraudulent in that pertinent facts and evidence had been willfully suppressed or omitted. It further stated that some of the orders of the decree went far beyond the complaint, and that there was no proof that whatever was shipped in interstate commerce was either "misbranded" or "adulterated." In other words, this brief rested its appeal on the legal aspects of the procedures, was worded in the usual legal terms, and still made the *mala fide* attitude of the prosecution quite clear. However, this appeal, too, was denied.

Still another brief was filed by Dr. Silvert, in which he referred not only to the fraudulent intent of the FDA, but to other aspects of the case not covered by the other briefs. He mentioned the personal funds given by Reich to the research work and showed the tactics of the accusers in their misrepresentation of the literature. Specifically, he pointed out that Reich's hardcover books were branded by the FDA as "labeling" for the accumulator and were destroyed, the allegations being that such books as *The Sexual Revolution; The Mass Psychology of Fascism; Character*

Analysis; Cosmic Superimposition; Ether, God and Devil; The Murder of Christ; and *People in Trouble* constitute "a claim of cure, mitigation, treatment of cancer." This appeal also was denied.

Thus, the law took its course and on March 12, 1957, twelve days before his sixtieth birthday, Reich entered the federal penitentiary in Danbury, Connecticut.

Prison Period

Reich remained in the Danbury Penitentiary for only ten days. There he underwent a psychiatric examination and was diagnosed as paranoid on the basis of his talks with the psychiatrist in which he mentioned the conspiracy against him on the part of Moscow and the Rockefellers, his contact with the U.S. Armed Forces, and the airplanes flying over the prison to protect and encourage him. The psychiatric report also stated: "The patient is relatively intact in the greater part of his personality. . . . In general his emotional responses and behavior are consistent with his ideas." The psychiatrist, who told me much later that he was very impressed by Reich and that he had great respect for him, suggested that Reich be transferred to Lewisburg which was the only federal penitentiary with psychiatric treatment facilities.

Reich was transferred to Lewisburg on March 22, but for several reasons no use was ever made of the treatment facilities. First, Reich himself refused absolutely any kind of psychiatric treatment, and second, the psychiatrists in Lewisburg—who I was given to understand agreed with the diagnosis—nevertheless decided to declare Reich legally sane and competent. It was explained to me that the reason for this was twofold: The psychiatrists did not feel that much could be gained by re-opening the entire case for reasons of legal insanity, and second, they felt that a man of Reich's standing should not be made to suffer from the label of legal insanity. I think this latter decision was an honorable one, and I am convinced that Reich himself would have fought very hard against re-opening the case with a plea of legal insanity.

On the other hand, the fact that he was declared legally sane and competent is being used quite often today by many of Reich's friends and co-workers in their insistence that all his decisions were perfectly sane. As I have said before, I am not psychiatrically trained and have to rely on experts in such matters, but I believe that nothing is taken from the greatness of the man and his accomplishments if one recognizes that some of his ideas of the 1950's were paranoid. Quite a few psychiatrists who were never inimical to Reich, who on the contrary are full of admiration, have concurred with the diagnosis of the prison psychiatrist in Danbury.

Reich was allowed correspondence with three persons and he chose his companion Aurora Karrer, his daughter Eva, and his son Peter. He also had these three persons on his visitors list, but as Peter was under fifteen years of age he could go there only when accompanied by one of the adults. For some reasons, neither Eva nor Miss Karrer could make it possible for Peter to visit his father more than twice, once at the end of May, and again at the beginning of October 1957. But the correspondence between Reich and Peter was very frequent and regular, and gives quite a few clues as to what Reich did, what his preoccupations were, and how he felt in prison.

We know that at times he worked in the prison library, that he did not have much contact with other prisoners, that he was writing a book on his mathematical orgonometric concepts although his notes were never found. Judging from normal prison routine one must conclude that all written material would have been destroyed by the authorities immediately after his death. Reich wrote in his letters that he read much, including Sandburg's four-volume Lincoln biography, and also Emerson's essays.

He wrote in the very beginning of his prison life, "I am taking it better than I thought I would," and again, in September, "Am doing well, much better than in Spring, though being here is bad enough."

Many of the letters repeated over and over: "I have won my battle!"

In May 1957 Reich started to set machinery in motion for a presidential pardon—which came to nought. He had hoped to be released on the basis of a pardon in May, and wrote about plans for the summer in Orgonon, or for a trip. He then had several meetings in prison with a lawyer from Washington with whom Eva worked on habeas corpus proceedings.

Reich was worried about the safety of all of us who had been involved in the trial, and told Peter to warn me to be careful, that Modju intended to destroy all of us, that his (Reich's) life was in grave danger. At about that time, in July, the idea appeared and re-appeared in his letters that one should look upon his being locked up as a protective measure. He mentioned once, "I carry two great secrets with me of which no one knows. One day the whole story will be told."

In one of the early letters to Peter, Reich said:

My present predicament is, in a way, an *honor,* since I am held here on the basis of an *unconstitutional,* i.e., *unlawful* court order. I am proud to be in the good, honorable company of Socrates, Christ, Bruno, Galileo, Moses, Savonarola, Dostojewski, Ghandi, Nehru, Minscenti, Nietzsche, Luther and many others who fought the devil of ignorance, unlawful acts of Government, social evil. . . . You know and have learned to trust in God as we have understood the *universal existence and rule of Life and Love.*

He wrote that he had attended in prison some Protestant church services: "I was deeply moved; I felt a new, *universal* faith in *Life and Love,* comprising all monotheistic beliefs, races, etc., is becoming a dire necessity to counter-weight and -act the 'Enemy of Man.' "

Many of his letters after this one showed a kind of religious fervor—somewhat difficult to understand in the man who for so many decades of his life had fought very articulately any kind of organized religion. He spoke about the need for "Harbors for Life," "Churches for Life," "Sanctuaries for Life." He told Peter not only to cry when the emotional pains became too hard to take, but to pray; he talked about the prayers he was composing and on June 14 he sent three of these prayers, entitled: "Resurrection = Life is Eternal, Indestructable;" "Prayer for Strength;" and "Prayer for Self-Realization." He also recommended to Peter on several occasions that he read the "Cadet's Prayer" which could be found in the army and navy hymn book.

I have not been able to understand this development in Reich as it seems so far removed from his thinking as I have known it. Maybe his Christ identification came into the picture here, the idea that he, too, would be crucified and that he was preparing a life-positive renewal of Christ's message of love, the beginning of which he had laid in his book *The Murder of Christ*.

In September Reich wrote that he was looking forward to talks with Peter at Christmas, outside of prison. Many of the letters hold great and lofty admonitions about truth, and the great line of life direction. These alternate with admonitions of a very practical nature: Don't be impertinent with teachers, obey the rules, always do your assigned work, study subjects even if you don't like them, and so on.

In the last letter Peter received from his father, on October 22, Reich wrote that he should know in about three weeks about his release, and that he was looking forward to the summer at Orgonon. In the same letter he mentioned the Sputnik, saying "Sputnik is a nice stunt, like a ball thrown upon ocean waves and tossed about helplessly. It will never be an active navigation vehicle. Ea (space ship run on orgone energy) is." He continued that a parole hearing was scheduled for November 5, and that he might be released possibly on November 10. He made a date with Peter at the Howard Johnson's Restaurant near his school in Poughkeepsie, and wanted him to find a small hotel there. He also mentioned plans for Thanksgiving dinner at Eva's house in Hancock.

Reich died in prison on November 3, 1957.

What we know about his last weeks is that he had felt sick for about two weeks prior to his death but did not want the prison authorities to know for fear that his sickness might hold up the parole. He intended to recuperate in a sanitarium after his release, and had friends make inquiries about a suitable place. There seems to be no doubt that he was fully aware of the seriousness of his heart condition.

It has often been maintained by friends of Reich that the prison authorities never knew of his bad heart. I have talked with the prison doctor who told me explicitly that the medical file very clearly indicated Reich's heart condition, although Reich had not mentioned his previous heart attack of 1951 to them. When I asked the physician whether this condition would not have been reason enough for a medical discharge, I was told that many prisoners with heart conditions are kept in prison because there is really no cure nor medication that would necessitate outside treatment.

The doctor also told me how Reich would pass through the doctor's office on his way to his daily bath, granted him because of his skin condition. Reich had asked this doctor to supply him with a commercial oil preparation for his skin because he felt that the prison pharmacist added something to the usual oil that was an irritant; the doctor gladly complied with this request. He told me that Reich would usually remain in the office for a short talk, and that all people in the office were much impressed by his knowledge and unquestionable genius. But they all felt strange when he would look up any time a plane flew overhead and say: "There they are, watching over me, encouraging me." The medical staff had no doubt that these were paranoid delusions in this otherwise superior and rational man.

I did not see the autopsy report but was told that it revealed the presence of broncho-pneumonia and hardening of the aorta. Upon special request a test was made for the presence of toxic substances, but the finding was negative. The death certificate stated that he had died of myocardial insufficiency with sudden heart failure associated with generalized arteriosclerosis and sclerosis of the coronary vessels.

Epilogue

Immediately after Reich's death, rumors started to fly everywhere that the judge had refused parole or that Reich had been poisoned in prison. It did not seem tragic enough to some people that he had died a martyr to his cause—they needed to blame some definite person or persons for his actual death.

The reaction to his death in the press was the same as had been given him in his lifetime. *The New York Times* had a short obituary note; *Time Magazine,* under "Milestones," reported on his death with some of the Brady article overtones; and some of the Maine daily papers had short obituaries. The *London Times* published an obituary, but both *The New Statesman* and the *Manchester Guardian* refused to publish a letter by Neill about Reich's death in prison. There were warm and touching reactions to Reich's death in the *Village Voice*.

I have indicated before that Reich was often preoccupied with the thought of what would happen to his remains when he died. He had made very definite arrangements for his funeral—down to the smallest details. He was to be buried at Orgonon, there was to be no religious ceremony, but he wanted the record of Schubert's *Ave Maria,* sung by Marian Anderson, to be played. He also ordered that his body be placed either under the front porch of the observatory—where his grave was put temporarily—or on the spot in the woods overlooking the mountains and lakes which he had previously designated and where the tomb now stands, covered at his request by a simple granite slab with only the words

WILHELM REICH
BORN MARCH 24, 1897 — DIED NOVEMBER 3, 1957

The bust made by Jo Jenks stands on top of it.

At the funeral, Dr. Elsworth Baker gave a brief eulogy, ending with Reich's version of the Lord's Prayer from his *Murder of Christ*.

The funeral was very much an extension of Reich's tragic life. There was already, before the funeral, a take over by a number of "pure Reichians" who wanted to exclude others from the funeral because Reich had not approved or completely trusted them. Many felt the irreplaceable loss of a leader, a teacher, a friend. But the atmosphere of the entire ceremony came very close to mass hysteria. The body had been brought from prison to Orgonon, accompanied by Miss Karrer and Eva. Upon Miss Karrer's orders the observatory was illuminated inside and outside all through the night before the funeral. The laboratory hall on the first floor served as funeral hall. The coffin was placed on one of the large laboratory tables, covered with the old Persian rug from Reich's library, and surrounded by flowers.

I was, no doubt, in a great emotional turmoil and very much concerned about Peter, but looking back at it now it appears to me that the hysterical element seemed to spread and obscure the true grief, the real loss and the tragic circumstances of the death.

There were—and to some extent still are—difficulties about

Reich's Last Will and Testament. It includes most of the usual legal phraseology, but contains as well many of Reich's theories and ideas in his own terminology which is so easily misinterpreted. Basically, with the exception of a few personal bequests, his entire estate was left to The Wilhelm Reich Infant Trust Fund which is to be administered by a single trustee.

Today, almost eleven years after his death, it seems that his often repeated thought that he would be appreciated by future generations is coming true. His books have been reissued here and abroad and are widely read. His psychiatric therapy is becoming more and more widely accepted. There are courses about Reich and his social and medical psychiatry taught at various outstanding universities. His biological and physical experiments continue here and there. And, as recently pointed out by Neal Ascherson in the London *Observer Review* of June 2, 1968, the work of Wilhelm Reich turns up everywhere. ". . . his fantastic synthesis of Freud and revolutionary politics, his account of the politically explosive nature of sexual relationships, his hypnotic diagrams showing sexual starvation leading to revolution, are squirted in paint on the Sorbonne walls or chucked at policemen's heads (in soft covers) by the free-living Communes of Berlin."

Maybe this is not quite the way he envisioned it, but it is a beginning. And although there is much antagonism among various schools of his former students and co-workers, each one claiming to be the true interpreter of Reich's work, the important thing seems to be that there are many young physicians, psychiatrists, biologists, and physicists continuing to work on the basis of Reich's findings. Therein lies the hope that some day soon his beloved Orgonon will cease to be a beautifully kept but sterile mausoleum and museum, and will instead be alive again with the humming activities of students eager to apply to living nature, to children, and to sick people all those findings of Reich's work which he himself dedicated to the "Children of the Future."

RANGELEY, MAINE, JULY 11, 1968

Selected Bibliography

By WILHELM REICH:

Der Triebhafte Charakter. Wien: Internationaler Psychoanalytischer Verlag, 1925.

Die Funktion des Orgasmus. Wien: Internationaler Psychoanalytischer Verlag, 1927.

Der Sexuelle Kampf der Jugend. Berlin: Sexpol Verlag, 1932.

Charakter-Analyse. Copenhagen: Sexpol Verlag, 1933.

Massenpsychologie des Faschismus, 2. Auflage. Copenhagen: Sexpol Verlag, 1933.

Dialektischer Materialismus und Psychoanalyse. Copenhagen: Sexpol Verlag, 1934.

Der Einbruch der Sexualmoral, 2. Auflage. Oslo: Sexpol Verlag, 1935.

Die Sexualität im Kulturkampf, 2. Auflage. Oslo: Sexpol Verlag, 1936.

Die Bione. Oslo: Sexpol Verlag, 1938.

The Sexual Revolution. New York: Orgone Institute Press, 1945; reissued in paperback by Farrar, Straus & Giroux, 1962.

The Mass Psychology of Fascism. New York: Orgone Institute Press, 1946.

The Cancer Biopathy. New York: Orgone Institute Press, 1948.

The Function of the Orgasm, 2nd Edition. New York: Orgone Institute Press, 1948; reissued by Farrar, Straus & Giroux, 1961.

Listen, Little Man! New York: Orgone Institute Press, 1948; reissued in paperback by Farrar, Straus & Giroux, 1965.

Character Analysis, 3rd Enlarged Edition. New York: Orgone Institute Press, 1949; reissued in paperback by Farrar, Straus & Giroux, 1961.

Ether, God and Devil. New York: Orgone Institute Press, 1949.

Cosmic Superimposition. Rangeley, Me.: The Wilhelm Reich Foundation, 1951.

The Oranur Experiment. Rangeley, Me.: Orgone Institute Press, 1951.

The Murder of Christ. Rangeley, Me.: Orgone Institute Press, 1953; reissued in paperback by Farrar, Straus & Giroux, 1956, 1966.

People in Trouble. Rangeley, Me.: Orgone Institute Press, 1953.

Selected Writings. New York: Farrar, Straus and Cudahy, 1960.

OTHER ORGONOMIC PUBLICATIONS:

International Journal of Sex-Economy and Orgone Research. New York: Orgone Institute Press, 1942-1945.

Annals of the Orgone Institute. New York: Orgone Institute Press, 1947.

Orgone Energy Bulletin. New York: Orgone Institute Press, 1949-1955.

Orgonomic Medicine. New York: Orgone Institute Press, 1955, 1956.

A. S. NEILL ET AL., Editor Paul Ritter. *Wilhelm Reich.* Nottingham: The Ritter Press, 1958.

ELSWORTH F. BAKER. *Man in the Trap.* New York: Macmillan Company, 1967.

MARY HIGGINS AND CHESTER M. RAPHAEL, M.D., ed. *Reich Speaks of Freud.* New York: Farrar, Straus & Giroux, 1967.

The Journal of Orgonomy. New York: Orgonomic Publications, 1967, 1968.

INDEX